The Handbook of College Student Excuses

David C. Wyld

Published by David Wyld, 2021.

While every precaution has been taken in the preparation of this book, the publisher assumes no responsibility for errors or omissions, or for damages resulting from the use of the information contained herein.

THE HANDBOOK OF COLLEGE STUDENT EXCUSES

First edition. March 10, 2021.

Copyright © 2021 David C. Wyld.

ISBN: 979-8224066506

Written by David C. Wyld.

To all my good students, for whom this does not apply...

The Handbook of College Student Excuses

The "Best" - *Well "Worst"* - Excuses Submitted by Students to Their Professors

David C. Wyld

The Handbook of College Student Excuses
The "Best" - Well "Worst" - Excuses Submitted
by Students to Their Professors
David C. Wyld

Copyright 2021 David C. Wyld

This ebook is licensed for your personal enjoyment only. This ebook may not be re-sold or given away to other people. If you would like to share this book with another person, please purchase an additional copy for each recipient. If you're reading this book and did not purchase it, or it was not purchased for your use only, then please purchase your own copy. Thank you for respecting the hard work of this author.

Acknowledgements

First off, let me say a heartfelt "thanks" to all of my colleagues from around the country who contributed their "best" excuses for this project. Literally, it would not exist without them having taken the time and effort to share their stories with me, so that I can share them with you in this book!

Next, I must express my love to my wife, Karla, who served as that "second set of eyes" in helping get this book into its final form. Now, in addition to all the hats that you have worn in the course of our lives together, you can add "editor" to that extensive list!

Let me also thank the two individuals whose work you see *visibly* in the book that you are about to read. The wonderful cover design came from Cal Sharp with Caligraphics[1]. I can't recommend him enough! The ebook was formatted with the assistance of Marti Dobkins of UCS Press[2]. If you're an experienced or aspiring book author, please contact her to help your work appear the very best it can be!

And finally yes, that memorable cover image - the smiling college grad who looks like he just might have used a few "creative" excuses on his professors during his time in school - came courtesy of a Pixabay user (robtowne0[3]), and it was sourced from him at: https://pixabay.com/photos/graduation-man-cap-gown-education-879941/.[4]

---

1.   https://www.caligraphicsdesign.com/

2.   https://www.ucspress.com/about-1.html

3.   https://pixabay.com/users/robtowne0-914531/

4.   https://pixabay.com/photos/graduation-man-cap-gown-education-879941/

Dedication

To my Dad, who taught me how to be a good manager, a good leader, a good father, a good husband, and most importantly, how to try to be a good guy overall (which may have led me to believe a few "questionable" student excuses over the years that I probably shouldn't have...)!

Preface

This book has simply been a joy for me to write and put together, and I sincerely hope that it will bring a bit of joy to you! We all need a little joy these days, as all of us continue to deal with the impact of the COVID-19 pandemic in our lives. And perhaps nowhere has the coronavirus had a more disruptive impact than in the world of higher education, forcing all of us - students, faculty, and yes, *even* administrators, to try and adapt to an ever-evolving "new normal" - *whatever* that might be at the moment! And so if my fellow faculty members and students alike can get a few chuckles out of reading this book, all the effort has been worth it!

Now this is a book that I never expected to write, but like so many things that prove beneficial in our lives and careers, it is nothing less than one of those "happy accidents" that propel us forward! As a management professor and consultant, I've made a career out of writing - *serious writing* - with hundreds of articles, white papers, book chapters and monographs on my vita. But this may be the project that I am most proud of, and who knows, it may turn out to be the one that for which I am most known! And if that's the case, I'll be very happy with the result of this "happy accident!" This book has been such a joy because of the topic - and how it came to be.

The book you are reading began as just a simple post that I made to a Facebook group for college faculty members, the Higher Ed Learning Collective[1]. One day while "working," I had seen a funny tweet about an outlandish student excuse about a student being late for a class because he had slipped on a corn dog! I made a quick post to this group, simply asking my fellow professors and instructors to post their "best" excuses that they had ever been presented with by their students.

---

1.   https://www.facebook.com/groups/onlinelearningcollective/

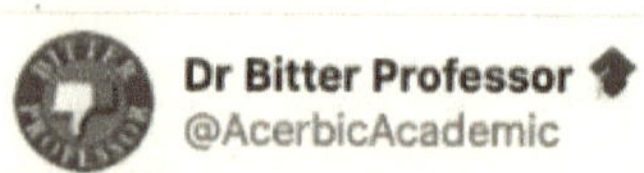

Source: Higher Ed Learning Collective (https://www.facebook.com/groups/onlinelearningcollective/permalink/744745959489438)

Wow! The responses started coming in quickly to my initial post, and then they kept on coming with my repost a few days later and the shares of both my posts in the Higher Ed Learning Collective! Suddenly I had *hundreds* of responses to my call for "best" excuses, and they were all very thoughtful, very interesting, and yes, alternately both very funny *and* somewhat scary at the same time!

I sensed that I had tapped into something more than just a social media discussion topic, and I reposted the post on a couple of other higher education Facebook groups and saw a similar reaction from my fellow college faculty members who freely shared their "best excuse" stories. I posted a similar call for "best excuses" on Twitter and saw even more great comments! That's when I knew that I had the makings for what I thought would be a "funny" journal article (not an oxymoron - and yes, they can *and* do exist!). However, when I began really combing through and collating all the great excuses that my contemporaries - over 500 college professors and instructors all over the country - had submitted, I saw the makings for a bigger project that became the book that you are about to read!

The excuses that you will soon read were so good and they spanned so many different areas - from health issues to tech problems to pets, family, travel and much, much more that I felt compelled to put this book together. I then spent many a day in my quarantined, "teaching from home" environment working with the excuse stories I received and weaved them into this book, and I am exceptionally proud of having done so! I truly hope that you will enjoy it and recommend it to your colleagues and heck, maybe even your students!

Now, I have been a college professor myself at a regional university in the South for almost thirty years. And in my time teaching there - at a school that is largely a commuter school and has a high percentage of both non-traditional and working students - I have seen and heard many interesting student excuses myself! And yes, while I've had some students that I know were likely either making up an excuse out of whole cloth or, at the very least, greatly embellishing their situation, I've also had quite the opposite. Indeed, I've had the honor of seeing students overcome whatever their circumstances - health, family, money, etc. - to do well in my classes.

And so that is the approach I am taking with this book, as while every chapter has many "best" excuses that we can laugh at, in almost every chapter, I also include stories submitted by my contemporaries of how their students have persisted and overcome the odds to do well in their courses! So yes, while the subtitle to this book shows that "best" has a double meaning when it comes to excuses (also meaning "worst"), we also see instances of the "best" of our students today. In no way then is this book meant to demean, make fun of, or "punch down" at college students. Rather, it is a crowdsourced look at the good, the bad, and the ugly of how student excuses work from both sides of the equation today!

So you might ask, why the title, "The Handbook of College Student Excuses?" Well, the obvious, "Seinfeldian-like" answer would be that. "Well, 'War and Peace' was already taken!" But seriously, this book is a compendium that should be of interest not just to my fellow university faculty, but to college students *and* maybe even their parents as well. So is it a handbook to follow? No. Is it a handbook of what not to do? Well, not entirely, as I explained just before this. Is it a handbook with answers (i.e. a "7 point plan to reduce fake excuses") to a "crisis" in terms of college student excuses? No, because on balance, I don't see a crisis. What I do see - and what my colleagues see every day - is that with more technology and resources than ever at students' disposal, excuses today are taking on new forms and branching into new categories. And yes, we now see students being *more creative than ever* before, and their excuses have more information - and sometimes *too much information* - to back them up!

And so I hope that you will kick back and simply enjoy the book you are about to read, perhaps with a good cup of coffee - or more - as you do! And if you enjoy this book, I hope that you will recommend it to your colleagues and maybe even your students! And yes, there could *very well* be a sequel, and if you'd like to contribute your "best" excuse for that, please contact me at dwyld@selu.edu. All excuses will be presented anonymously as they have been in this book, even to the point of masking the identity of the university involved if that was made obvious in the excuse story. I truly look forward to hearing from you with your own "best" excuse story - or stories if you will, as well as your feedback on this unique book.

And so with that being said, I hope that you enjoy this labor of pandemic love that I put together - "The Handbook of College Student Excuses."

Chapter 1: Overview

Introduction

In this book, we will explore the "best" - well, read that as the *worst* - excuses offered by college students for missing classes, tests, paper due dates, etc. The basis of the book has been "crowdsourced," as college professors from around the country responded to an invitation on social media to share their most memorable excuses offered by their students over the course of their teaching careers. The book has been compiled and authored by Dr. David C. Wyld, himself a business professor with over thirty years of classroom experience. While prior to this project, he might have thought that he had seen it all, the feedback Dr. Wyld got from hundreds of professors for this project shows just how unlucky, how creative, and yes, sometimes just how inspiring a student excuse can be!

This book, with contributions from over 500 college professors and instructors from all over the country, should be of interest to many different audiences, including university administrators, college faculty, *and yes*, college students (and maybe even their parents)! Indeed, today's students might be able to learn from the "lessons learned" by prior students in their interactions with their professors, and see how excuses - of all types - are viewed from the other side of the equation.

Now, I have to begin this book with a disclaimer: Professors are by and large a *very empathetic* bunch of people. After all, we have made a career choice to work with college students and help advance their development, education, and careers. But still, like you, we can laugh at a whole host of excuses students have tried - *and* in many cases succeeded - in convincing their college instructors that they had a legitimate excuse for being absent, for missing a test, for not making a presentation, or for not being able to turn a paper in on time.

Yes, many of these student excuses chronicled in this book will have you staring at the screen in disbelief and even laughing out loud at their absurdness (and a warning that more than a few of these excuses perhaps might even have you spitting your coffee out on your device's screen!). While some of these excuses offered by students - well, *more than a few* - are highly creative and fantastical in nature, sometimes as we all know, the unlikely and improbable *does* happen. Take for instance this post from a colleague somewhere in the United States (and yes, I promised anonymity to all who contributed their student excuses for this project):

- *"My first year teaching I had a student miss the first test telling me her mom had died. The second test came along and I got a phone message saying she had been in a car accident. For the third test, she came to my office to say her husband had just been diagnosed with cancer and she couldn't concentrate. I don't ask for documentation and tend to take people at their word, but I called bullshit. I have never felt like less of a human being than when I found out it was all true...."*

And speaking of death, here's an excuse submitted by one of my contemporaries with an amazing - but true - student story:

- *"I don't know about my worst one (excuse), but I do have the best one... one of my students was late to class one morning because SHE DIED. Literally. She has a congenital heart defect and had to be rushed to the hospital where they revived her during the night. And she still showed up the next morning... just late."*

Excuses, Excuses, Excuses

While we may laugh at some very questionable student excuses throughout this book, just know that *all of this* is offered in a good spirit. In no way are these excuses being offered by my colleagues and highlighted here intended to be "punching down" or belittling students in any way. And know this: There *are* tremendously dedicated students out there in the student body - *always*. And sometimes, we see students in fact go way, *way* beyond what anyone would expect. Take for instance the story related by one of my contemporaries about a pregnant student:

- *"I had a student in labor. The doctor told her it would probably be awhile. She came to class (having contractions) and took a final. Then went back to the hospital and had the baby! She even had the hospital band on her wrist! And she had one of the highest grades on the final!"*

Sometimes though, all of us get the *very real* student stories that can lead us to share a tear or two ourselves, as students today *do* have hardships that many of us cannot simply imagine - and these date back long before COVID-19. Take this professor's story for instance:

- *"I had a student arrive late with a note from her kids explaining that they were hungry and asked her to make dinner first. I still have that note on my bulletin board."*

There are, however, the student excuses that are, well, mind-boggling in their absurdity - *and* in their improbability:

- *"One of my students was late to the class video meeting because he was eating cake in the shower and it fell and plugged the drain so his shower started flooding and his mom came upstairs because there was water flooding the kitchen. I am not sure how cake would plug a drain to the point one couldn't just clear it out, but his mom was yelling at him about cake in the background so I believed him...and laughed for about ten minutes!"*

- *"Student says his aunt gives him medicine that makes him spacey, so it makes him forget to do his work. It was Metamucil!"*

- *"Students said: 'I thought I was dying and went to urgent care but my tongue was blue because of a lollipop.' Got that one in an email 8 years ago that's still in my 'Keep' folder."*

- *"A local student submitted an assignment an hour late and said she didn't know what time zone we lived in...all semester."*

And yes, while there's no proven scientific theory behind this, one can safely say that the intricacy of a student excuse might just be inversely related to just how much truth there might be contained within it, as this one enterprising student's excuse shows:

- *"I passed by my student on the way to class and he told me he was getting coffee and then coming to class. He asked me if I wanted one, and I said no thanks. Class started and I didn't see him. 20 minutes into class another student's phone rings and he answered it. He told me it was for me. It was the student who I passed on the way to class. He told me after he bought coffee, he went home to get his backpack. (He had his backpack on when I passed him). Then he said when he got home, his dog destroyed everything in his apartment and he had to clean up. Once he finished cleaning up, he left to head back to campus to join the class. Unfortunately, he stepped in a giant puddle and his clothes got soaked, so he had to turn back to change. (It was over a hundred degrees that day and not a cloud in the sky). Once he got back he realized, by the time he would dry up, it would be too late to go to class. So he asked me to mark him as if he attended, because if none of that happened he would have come to class. I was floored with this excuse. I was silent, rolled my eyes, and hung up the phone. True story!"*

Then there is this story from an anonymous colleague, which reads almost like an excuse developed by the student in the spirit of *"If You Give a Mouse a Cookie[1]"*:

- *"I had a student drop off the face of the earth for two months only to return two weeks before the end of the semester wanting to make up all the labs. When I refused, telling her that what she requested was too much work for her to succeed, she told me I couldn't refuse her because she was out due to a heart condition. When I asked why she didn't email, she said she couldn't because she had to stay flat on her back. When I asked why she didn't dictate an email to someone who could type it for her, she got pushy. When I asked why she didn't call me to inform me, she repeated that she had to stay flat on her back, to which I replied, 'The phone still works no matter which way you are holding it.'"*

---

1.   *https://www.amazon.com/You-Give-Mouse-Cookie-Book/dp/0060245867*

One of my colleagues even asked her students to come-up with the "most absurd" excuse they could as a creative exercise, and this is "the best one" that she received in return:

- *"One semester when I was teaching deviance I told students in that class to come up with the most outlandish excuses they could and I'd announce the "ridiculous excuse winner" at the end of the semester. Only one student gave a non-normative excuse that entire semester and it was, 'Aliens kidnapped me to teach them out to hunt during the opening week of deer season.'"*

And then again, there are excuses that sound incredible (and entries into the previous professor's contest!) - but they are in fact *very* real:

- *"'I couldn't finish my essay last night because I had to go bail Grandpa out of jail.' And it turned out to be true."*

- *"Ok this one was actually true, though it sounds fake. A student called me (knowing I'd never believe an email) that she couldn't get out of her house to come to class because there was a mountain lion on her porch! (It's Colorado, so this stuff happens haha)!"*

- *"I always appreciate an excuse from a student that I haven't heard before because they are so crazy they have to be true. I once had a student borrow a Post-It Note poster pad for a class presentation. He came to me later and confessed that he could not return it because his roommate had been drinking and when my student suggested slowing down, the roommate sped up in protest, got sick, and puked all over it. He didn't think I would want it back (which I agreed!) and he offered to buy me a new one. I told him that the story alone was worth the replacement cost!"*

- *"Once had a student claim a dead grandma three times in one semester. I can't remember the specific circumstances, but it turned out to be true!"*

But every once in a while, some of us do encounter a student who just "throws him or herself on the mercy of the court" with an honest, "non-excuse excuse":

- *"I had a student email me: 'I have no good excuse and I'd rather not have to explain my bad reasons. I will turn in all of my late assignments by the end of the week. If you have time to evaluate them I'd appreciate feedback, even though I don't expect to receive credit.' I appreciated their honesty and humility!"*

And so, as we look at a whole host of excuses from students, offered by professors from colleges and universities all around the country, do know that *all of this* is offered in a good spirit, as we have *all* been there ourselves! We have all been in a pinch sometime - and maybe *many* sometimes - in the course of our lives where we face a conundrum: Do we tell the truth, *or* do we construct a lie? Whether it was in our own college days, on the job, or in a relationship (or perhaps "all of the above!"), we've all - and yes, some of us many, *many* times - had to decide on whether to level with another person as to what was really going on in our lives or to construct a story from "alternative facts." In this book, we will see a mix of both - we will see excuses that are too fanciful to be true *and* those that are true despite seeming to be too fanciful to possibly be true - *but they are*!

Overview of the Book

And so this book explores the *"best"* (really meaning the *"worst"*) college student excuses of all time. *All* of these excuses came from my contemporaries who are professors and instructors all over America, each of whom responded to a social media invitation to submit their "best" excuses offered by their students for missing a class, a test, a project due date, etc. In all, over 500 higher education faculty from across the United States ended up submitting excuses that spanned the gamut in terms of their "origins" - health conditions, tech issues, legal problems, social and family issues, pet and animal concerns, housing issues, and much, much more.

This book, "crowdsourced" from my contemporaries' very generous (and anonymous) submissions of their "best" student excuses, explores just how far students will go to craft excuses that will convince their college instructors to excuse an absence, let them take a make-up test, turn a paper or project in late, etc. And yes, we may laugh at the absurdity of many of these excuses. However, in almost every instance, there were also examples provided by my colleagues around the country of students who persevered, overcoming whatever obstacle that was in their way to make it to class, to complete the paper on-time, or yes, to take a test while in active labor!

You can say one thing about all of the hundreds of excuses submitted from my fellow college faculty members. While sometimes we professors hear or read "TMI" (*too much information*) about a student's excuse, perhaps it is just a sign - and yes, a *positive* sign - about today's students. As one of my colleagues put it so well:

- *"I think that students, particularly Gen Z students (those born after 1997), are somewhat comfortable being honest about why they missed class or an assignment and are just telling us, but they aren't using it as an 'excuse' in that they don't expect to be legitimately excused from class, or they expect a late penalty of some kind. I've had students tell me they just needed a personal day and wanted to let me know why they were gone because they cared about the class. When I get those kinds of emails, that's how I take it. If they didn't care about my class, they would have just skipped and not reached out at all."*

So, I would encourage you to kick back with a good cup of coffee (or more) as you read through the chapters that follow. You will laugh at many of these excuses, and yes, in some instances, you may be inspired and even shed a tear or two!

Chapter 2: The "Death Card"

Let's begin our exploration of student excuses by looking at what is perhaps the *ultimate* card that a student has to play when it comes to being absent from a class, missing a test, or failing to meet a deadline. It is the *"Death Card."*

The Death Card

Now to begin, death is - as they say - *really* no laughing matter. And as faculty, we know that students will unfortunately experience losses of people near and dear to them during the course of a semester. We know that such a loss can not just make completing the course more difficult for a student, but more importantly, make their life more difficult. That is why to a person, I feel that almost every college faculty member will go out of their way to work with students who experience the death of a loved one while taking their class. Death and loss are something that all of us "of a certain age" can unfortunately empathize with *very well*, as we have most assuredly experienced the loss of family members and friends in our own time.

Yet, professors also have to deal with the flip side of the "Death Card," and that is the fact that there *are* some students who will use a fake death story as an excuse for them to use for a missed class, test, project deadline, etc. How frequently this is done can't really be quantified, of course. But yes, it's an old adage among faculty members that exam time is especially risky for grandmothers - and for other family members as well (but especially for grandmas - *not* grandpas!). There's even a famous satirical study done on the matter, entitled "The Dead Grandmother/Exam Syndrome and the PotentialDownfall Of American Society[1]," with the classic thesis statement:

---

1.   https://devblogs.microsoft.com/oldnewthing/20140113-01/?p=2093

"The basic problem can be stated very simply: A student's grandmother is far more likely to die suddenly just before the student takes an exam, than at any other time of year."

The author of The Dead Grandmother/Exam Syndrome study concluded that we simply had to stop giving exams in college, as there was simply *too high* a correlation between a student having a test and grandma dying! And one of my anonymous colleagues freely admitted:

- *"I personally killed my whole family at least 10 times while I was an undergrad."*

The extreme risk to close family members around exams, paper deadlines, presentation dates, etc. was proven true by the many responses received regarding students playing the "Death Card" - sometimes *even repeatedly* during the same semester with the same professor!

- *"Ha! I teach English Composition, which is the Number One killer of Grandmas. Some of them die more than once in the same semester."*

- *"I don't know. I teach Anatomy & Physiology. I have killed a shit tonne of relatives. At least eight each semester."*

- *"Between a colleague and I, one student in our classes had six grandparents die over two semesters."*

- *"At my colleague's last school, they called graduation 'Resurrection Day.'"*

Don't have an obituary or a funeral card/program for a death excuse? This is not an issue for some students:

- *"One girl told me that she missed my exam because her mother died. I offered condolences and requested documentation. An obituary would do. Two days later I came to campus and found a note slipped under my office door. It was a pencil-written letter in girly cursive written on a page torn out of a spiral notebook stating that the girl's mother had died. It was signed "xxxx's father."*

Sometimes though, students do experience the "Revenge of the Dead" - *for real*:

- *"Oh, I had an epic 'dead grandma' story. I received a call from a student the night before the exam (I gave out my number for emergencies) and he gave me this horrible story about his beloved grandmother dying and he just couldn't function and really needed an extension on the exam. What said student didn't know was that both Grandma and I were from the same town. And it just so happened that at the time of this call, I was sitting at the same table with her at a church event. I responded to him by name, saying I was so sorry that his Grandma Beth died. Grandma Beth, who is one sharp cookie, took one look at me and said, 'Is that _____?' Before I could finish nodding, she ripped the phone out of my hand, stalked off to an empty classroom, and proceeded to give her grandson one HECK of a chewing out. She returned about twenty minutes later, handed my phone back to me, and said, 'He WILL be in class tomorrow.' The next morning, he was twenty minutes early and gave me flowers as an apology for his lying and that he 'would never do this again.'"*

- *"When I was in grad school, an undergrad ended up facing disciplinary actions because she told her professor she would miss an exam because her father died. The professor felt horrible that she would have such an experience as losing her father, so she got the student's home number and called to give their condolences. The father answered the phone."*

And yes, students may be surprised to learn that sometimes, they can play the "Death Card" one too many times:

- *"Had a student walk in my office crying that her mother died and asked if I would work with her. Well yes, obviously. She walks out of my office and another instructor walks in my office and says did her mother die again this semester? That was many years ago. I now require an obituary or service program."*

- *"The student who claimed dead grandma... as they had every semester for the previous three years. Apparently, they thought professors don't chat."*

- *"One time, a student of mine had his Aunt pass away. I obviously said no worries hand it in when you could. About 2-3 months later, I was sitting down for lunch with other faculty members on the program ... and one of my colleagues told us to keep an eye on the student because he had an aunt pass away. I asked if it was the same aunt from 2-3 months ago. By the end of the conversation, we realized that over the past two years he had roughly 7 aunts pass away."*

It is important however to recognize that a student using a false death of a family member as an excuse *can be quite painful* for the faculty member on the other end of the transaction - especially at certain times for all of us. This was exemplified by this submission from an anonymous colleague:

- *"I had a kid lie to me about the death of his father once. It was especially awful since the class was aware that my own father had just died over break."*

Now sadly, most of the time, of course, when students play the "Death Card' *it is legitimate* in that they truly have experienced the loss of a loved one or even a close friend. And yes,

sometimes the "Dead Grandma" stories are indeed true - even if they are statistically unlikely if they become *"Dead Grandmas"* stories:

- *"Once had a student claim a dead grandma three times in one semester. I can't remember the specific circumstances, but it turned out to be true!"*

Conclusion

Now while we may laugh at some of these death-related excuses for their statistical unlikelihood *and* their absurdity, we all know that there are also excuses in this realm that are *both* absolutely true and in many cases, positively inspiring.

And so in dealing with death issues, there can also be stories of family tragedies that are indeed incredible, but sadly true as well, such as this one offered up by a colleague:

- *"I once had a student who called me and said, 'I know I have no excuse and no right to ask for an extension because I have missed so much class, but I have been keeping up with the reading and I think I can do a good job on the paper.' I encouraged her to tell me what was going on and this was her story: She had a nine month old baby, and her grandmother who had raised her died shortly after the birth. She decided that she would hire a private detective to find out what happened to her Mom who disappeared when she was in elementary school. It took the detective 2 weeks to find her mother's body in the basement of an abandoned house not far from where they lived when she was a kid. Her mother and another woman had been murdered and their bodies were in this abandoned house for like 10 years. She finished by saying, 'I know it is no excuse, but I have had trouble concentrating. I don't want you to think I don't care about your class.' To say that I was humbled at that moment is an understatement."*

Sometimes, in the wake of suffering a significant loss of someone close to them, students will persevere and still do very well on the task at hand, whether that be taking a test, turning in a paper, making a presentation, etc. This makes them inspirational stories, as in this instances relayed by these contemporaries:

- *"I had a student find out the morning of the final that her father died. She took the final anyway. I was amazed at how composed she was. She ended up doing fairly well. I would have given her an incomplete and let her take it the next semester, but she didn't even ask. She just didn't want something else worrying her."*

- *"I teach at a Federal Service Academy, so my students are all military members. I believe I actually broke down in tears when a student 'respectfully requested' an extension on a paper because a parent had passed and they were requesting emergency leave to attend the funeral. Dear Lord, the parent in me wanted to reach out and hug them!"*

Chapter 3: The Medical File

In this chapter, we continue our exploration of student excuses by looking at health issues, which are unquestionably *the* most common reason students really legitimately miss a class, a test, or a deadline - *and* the one they go to most often if they were to want to fabricate an excuse for themselves.

Medical Excuses

Now when it comes to medical excuses, one professor expressed a sentiment that we *all* share when it comes to health issues...

- *"I've had students offer to show me wounds/injuries. Uh, I teach MATH, so I DO NOT want to see!"*

And yes, sometimes - well many times - we get TMI (too much information) from students when trying to justify their health-based excuse:

- *"'Sorry I had to miss class as I was getting my tattoo removed.' Photo included in the email message..."*

- *"I had a student miss multiple classes because of back problems. I was discussing her issues and she said, 'it's because, umm...' she points to her chest, 'my boobs are too big.' That is just not a problem I can relate to!"*

- *"I had one guy call me in class to say that he was at the STD clinic so could not make it....and so was another student in the class."*

- *"I had a student tell me he smoked too much weed. I appreciated the honesty."*

- *"Sorry I missed class. I was having my foot tattoo removed. Picture was attached of a half removed tattoo."*

- *"A student emailed me to tell me he was type 1 diabetic and he was having a really hard time managing his sugar that day and felt terrible. Fine, totally excusable. But he sent me a picture of the pee strip to prove his ketones were low!"*

- *"I had one email that he missed class because the night before he got drunk, tried to jump a fence, and broke his face. He then attached a picture of his bruised and bloody face."*

- *"Sorry I missed class for a week. I went to a different state to donate my eggs."*

- *"I had a student who missed a couple labs because he got hit by a train. He was putting pennies on the tracks and a bar sticking out from the train hit him in the head and knocked him out, and his hand landed on the rail and he lost most of his fingers. I'll never forget when he came back and told us - and showed us!"*

- *"I had a student send me photos of their vomit to prove they were really sick."*

- *"'I couldn't afford my meds, I got into a fight and got stabbed'—he also came back to class too early and had to run out of the room because his wound started to bleed. He offered to show me, I passed on that opportunity."*

- *"I have received pictures of rashes and infections, one clearly in the pubic region. I now explicitly tell students that I do not require any documentation for absences or make-up work."*

- *"I have chlamydia!"*

- *"Okay, this one left me speechless, but I had a student email to tell me that she missed classes because she has a yeast infection and can't wear any underwear. TMI for sure!"*

Medical issues can run the gamut, and *literally*, either the most absurd *and* unlucky things happen to students, or alternatively, students can just be darn creative in concocting their own health-related excuses:

- *"I had one student show up in my office with oozing sores all over to let me know that he had foot and mouth disease. Thanks!"*

- *"Student says his aunt gives him medicine that makes him spacey, so it makes him forget to do his work. It was Metamucil."*

- *"Student said: 'I thought I was dying and went to urgent care but my tongue was blue because of a lollipop.' Got that one in an email 8 years ago that's still in my 'Keep' folder."*

- *"A student missed a test after a run-in with a bat necessitated rabies shots."*

- *"I had a student who opened the cabinets in her kitchen, and a baking sheet fell out and hit her on the head! The student was fine, just wanted to take the test later!"*

- *"I had one who said he missed class because his hemorrhoids were really bad. I'm not saying it wasn't true, but I definitely wanted the brain bleach after getting that message."*

- *"Student emailed me that 'he couldn't come to class because of allergic reaction to pumpkin beer.'"*

- *"A few years ago, the female students in my department liked to tell my senior male colleague that they had to miss class 'for female problems.' Now, I understand bad cramps—but they NEVER gave me that explanation for absences!"*

- *"Student didn't finish the final project because they were "hungry and sleepy AF."*

Of all student activities, skateboarding seems to be the one that brings about the most interesting - and some of the most painful (*literally!*) - excuses.

- *"I had one student who was skateboarding to get a coffee, crashed, and ended up with a concussion. They ended the email with 'and I never got the coffee.'"*

- *"A student walked into class 15 minutes late actively bleeding with a huge gash on his elbow and his skateboard in hand. So casually he said 'sorry I am late—I got hit by a car on the way to class.' I just stopped mid lecture and was like 'omg do you need to see a doctor!?' Gotta give him props for still coming (and yes I told him to leave and go to the health center.)"*

And there are those students with medical issues that just make you go, "why?":

- *"'I can't come to class for the next week because I have a severe concussion from trying to open a can of cinnamon rolls with my head.'*

And yes, one person's perception of severity and relatedness can be quite different from another's.

- *"My brother had to go get a dangerous shot."*

- *"I had a student miss the midterm because he had an in-grown toenail."*

- *"'I couldn't type because I have a torn ACL in my elbow.' (My fave!)"*

Sometimes, a student's medical excuse can even be a learning experience and make one more "hip" and knowledgeable of youth slang today - I know this one was for me!:

- *"This is actually an example of an instance that illustrates my lack of knowledge of popular culture/slang etc. and I do not think it is an unreasonable reason from my student. The student waited after class and walked out of the classroom with me. Once in the hallway, they said that they were sorry that they missed class, but it was "shark week." I thought they meant the TV programming. Luckily, another student was there and they chimed in about how terrible their shark week is, and eventually I realized it was a metaphor. . . .Later, I heard the reference in a TV show and felt *hip*, because I knew what it meant. Thanks, student."*

And yes, I too thought this excuse was about "shark week" on TV, as in well, "sharks." However, upon further review and consulting with the Urban Dictionary[1], "shark week[2]" today can be a label for having your period, as in: *"the week a woman experiences menstruation; Shannon was in a bad mood because it was shark week."*

Finally, there is this story from an anonymous colleague, which reads almost like a medical excuse fused with the logic of *"If You Give a Mouse a Cookie[3]"*:

---

1.   https://www.urbandictionary.com/

2.   https://www.urbandictionary.com/define.php?term=shark%20week

- "I had a student drop off the face of the earth for two months only to return two weeks before the end of the semester wanting to make up all the labs. When I refused, telling her that what she requested was too much work for her to succeed, she told me I couldn't refuse her because she was out due to a heart condition. When I asked why she didn't email, she said she couldn't because she had to stay flat on her back. When I asked why she didn't dictate an email to someone who could type it for her, she got pushy. When I asked why she didn't call me to inform me, she repeated that she had to stay flat on her back, to which I replied, 'The phone still works no matter which way you are holding it.'"

Gastrointestinal Issues

Stomach issues deserve a category unto themselves, as not just simply having an upset stomach or a "stomach bug," but specifically, throwing-up and having "active" diarrhea seem to be the "go to" excuses for many students. And if there is a leading cause of student absences when it comes to health, gastrointestinal issues certainly lead the way (and again, many will provide *way too much* information on what caused them to get sick!).

- "I had a student miss a class due to, and I quote, 'extreme bowel movements.' I didn't ask for details...just replied 'okay.'"

- "In grad school, my first professor specifically told students not to eat convenience stores hot dogs on exam day. Grad school, public health... Students should have figured this out on their own."

- "Student missed an in-person exam due to eating a bad burrito. Unfortunately, they provided GRAPHIC detail about the digestive consequences of said burrito."

- "I could not write the exam because I had severe diarrhea. #tmi"

---

3.   *https://www.amazon.com/gp/product/0060245867/*

ref=as_li_tl?ie=UTF8&camp=1789&creative=9325&creativeASIN=0060245867&linkCode=a

s2&tag=ideapublishin-20&linkId=c2b44b13610001f68a6cb27f1d0f9306

- "Diarrhea. Offered to send time-stamped photos as evidence. On the flip side, I had a student who had been shot in the head check out of the hospital to come to class, despite my encouragement to take time to heal. (That student kinda ruined it for any other student, to be honest.)"

- "My Japanese students have been known to tell me they were suffering from 'sushi bowels.'"

Catching Students in a Health Lie

Of course, not every medical excuse *is* real. As a professor, you know that, and yes sometimes you do see evidence of such with your own eyes:

- "Probably 20 years ago I received a phone call from a student who claimed to be in a cardiac intensive care unit. He claimed to be hooked to life support and heart monitor. The beeping sound of the heart monitor was a friend doing a bad imitation of a heart monitor. I could also hear faint giggling in the background. The student never returned to class after that."

- "I had a student submit a handwritten note to excuse 2 weeks' worth of absences. The note was in pencil, had several mis-spellings, and looked like a 7-year-old wrote it, but this student claimed it was from his doctor. The wacky thing was he was also attending my husband's class during that time and of course, he tried to pull it on him as well - so a 'two fer!'"

- "I had a student email me that he was rushed to the hospital for not feeling well... as I watched him play monopoly in the student union while I grabbed a coffee on break. This was the same student who handed in a plagiarized paper on Cats, the musical. The copy/paste was obvious because he had copied the material from the musical's website, but included a link not to it, but to "Cats on Broadway," a veterinary hospital in Missoula, Montana."

- "I once received an absence note from 'Dr. Martin Lawrence.' (This was in the 90's, so he [Martin Lawrence] was on TV and all.) Just for

giggles, I drove by the building that was supposed to be his office, just in case there really was a doctor with that name. Nope."

- "I was on my way to the classroom to give an exam, and a student called and told me he was at the hospital with his girlfriend, who, he said, 'was having an abortion at that minute.' He was however, standing outside the classroom building as I walked in to give the exam."

- "I had a student miss a test because his grandfather was in the hospital. Of course I excused and let him make up the exam at a later date. However, turns out the student was the brother of a friend of mine and when I asked her about her grandfather, she had no idea what I was talking about..."

- "In the early days of Facebook, a student missed a majority of my class and at the end of the semester, wanted an incomplete. She had gained the confidence of the assistant department chair, who scheduled a meeting where they were to make the case that the student had a mental health problem and should be excused from having missed all but 4 classes, and should be allowed to turn in the assignments sometime later (never mind this is a lab-based course with a field placement). Prior to the meeting, I looked her up on Facebook, only to find a fully public profile with hundreds of photos of her, underage drinking and partying across the country—on days when class was scheduled. In the meeting, I listened to the sad story of how she couldn't even get out of bed most days. I listened to the case from the administrator. Then I asked them both to put themselves in my shoes and consider how that explanation compared to what she's putting on Facebook. I had printed out her profile and set in on the table in front of her. That ended the meeting pretty quickly."

- "I had a student say that they were going to submit an assignment late because they were volunteering with a kid with cancer and then proceeded to provide me with extremely personal information about this child (who was in no way related to them) in a way that read to me like they were simply trying to tug at heartstrings and to also make themselves look superior as a person who volunteers with kids with cancer. I found

it absolutely disgusting. Submitting the assignment late wasn't a big deal for me, and I granted the extension, but the exploitation of a child really pissed me off."

Then there's this classic regarding a dental excuse, with a comment from the dentist involved that was spot-on:

- "*I had a student forge dental notes to excuse absences. Multiple days (not consecutively), and the dentist was a couple of hours away. When I called the dentist to confirm, he remarked, 'If the student worked as hard in the class as he did to fake these notes, he would probably be doing a lot better in the course.' Student ended up expelled.*"

And for some reason, there seems to be some *very real* confusion as to the nature of prostate cancer among some male students out there!

- "*There was one time that a student told me he couldn't make the exam because his grandmother had prostate cancer. I just stared at him blinking for a looooong time...*"

- "*My favorite of all time happened to a colleague. A female prof had a male student tell her that he had gone home because his mom had cancer. Being a compassionate person, she asked him more about the situation. He volunteered that his mom had prostate cancer. She suggested that his mom might want to get a second opinion!*"

Finally though, here is an excuse from one of my colleagues that captures just how much many of us in the professoriate want to believe our students when it comes to medical-related issues, but sometimes, there are indeed signs that we shouldn't:

- "*First, I do have a tendency to believe people too often. Second, I was new to the Mayo Clinic area in Rochester, Minnesota. They do a lot of amazing things at the Mayo Clinic. This student told me that her husband was having a trans-species transplant. I believed her. It wasn't true. However, that was at least 22 years ago. I'm going to guess that maybe that could happen today, LOL.*"

Conclusion

Now while we may laugh at some of these health-related excuses for their statistical unlikelihood and their absurdity, we all know that there are also excuses in this realm that are *both* absolutely true and in many cases, positively inspiring.

Of course, for all the seemingly absurd - and yes, sometimes questionable - health-related excuses we professors receive from students to try and justify an absence, a missed test, or a past due assignment, there are those students who persevere over their medical concerns, like these:

- *"I had a student who came in halfway through an exam because he hit himself in the face with his car door. The poor guy was rushing from a rotation at a hospital across town, got out of the car, and somehow cut himself on the corner of the car door as he was getting out. He was excused and I took him to the ER. He needed three stitches."*

- *"I actually had a former student have some weird freak accident while packing to move and stabbed herself in the eye with a half inch auger. She is blind in that eye now. Still got a 4.0 that semester and is kicking ass in PA (Physicians Assistant) school. But holy crap!"*

- *"One of the strangest excuses I ever heard for not turning in that week's work (after they were a stellar straight-A student all semester, mind you) was that they'd severed their feet - technically their toes, I guess. The strangest part of the excuse was it was for real. They had had to get their feet surgically put back together after a ladder had broken and came down, the rungs mangling their feet at the arches. My poor student had been in the hospital and unconscious the entire week, so hadn't had a chance to even tell me they'd be late. When they finally woke up, the first thing they told their spouse was to contact me to say their work would be late that week. I told them to take two weeks, at least! Their adviser called me to say they had a doctor's note if I needed it as proof and I said not to worry about it, I believed them.*

It is always amazing to see how pregnant students manage to take classes while they are expecting (and BTW, my university does not have desks that are in *any way* friendly to expectant mothers!), and especially those who have a baby during the course of the semester - and finish classes successfully. There are, of course, a lot of situations that can *and do* happen with pregnant students, and among them are some truly incredible stories about women taking tests while in labor!:

- *"One of my coworkers had a situation where a student's water broke during an exam and she adamantly insisted that 'it wasn't going to be that fast' and she was going to finish the final. My coworker had to work really hard to get her to accept transportation to the hospital and taking the exam later (it had just started and was a 3-hour final exam period)."*

- *"One of my best students emailed me and said that she might be a few hours late with her assignment submission because she was in labor! I told her not to worry about it! She ended up submitting her paper on time and then she sent me a baby picture the next day! Amazing!"*

- *"I had a student take a final exam while in labor. She said it was her third she'd be fine, she'd just finish the exam and <u>then</u> go to the hospital."*

- *"I had a student in labor. The doctor told her it would probably be 'awhile.' She came to class (having contractions) and took a final. Then went back to the hospital and had the baby! She even had the hospital band on her wrist! And she had one of the highest grades on the final!"*

- *"Happy extreme: We actually had a write up in the newspaper of one of our students (at Middle Georgia State University[4]) doing her final exam online while in labor in the hospital. It went viral! (See: 'Unstoppable! New mom explains why she took a college exam during labor[5]')"*

There are students who have to be talked out of doing things they think they need to do for their classes for the "bigger picture" of their

---

4.   *https://www.mga.edu/*

5.   *https://www.today.com/parents/unstoppable-new-mom-explains-why-she-took-college-exam-during-t57226*

own health, and sometimes, that's where us professors come in to act all *in loco parentis* for them, as in this instance:

- *"I had a student show up with the hospital bracelet still on his wrist and his discharge papers hot off the presses in hand. I told him to go home and we would sort out the rest later."*

And then, there are students with medical issues that can be downright inspiring!

- *"Student emailed me that she was missing class for surgery to give a kidney to her father."*

- *"Student gave 1/2 of his liver to his brother..."*

- *"I had a student who suddenly went blind and was hospitalized while they tried to figure out what happened. I worked with his mother and he dictated his work to her and we got him through the class. He also was on the autism spectrum and his mom thanked me for working with her son. I told her I raised a son with Asperger's so I understand!"*

- *"I had a student who was hospitalized (immunosuppressed for cancer treatment) show up with a pile of all the homework they'd missed during the weeks they were out, most of it right. I found they'd been working with the textbook and a tutor over the phone (was before videochats were widely available). Impressed as hell! I would've supported a medical withdrawal or incomplete, but they didn't want to go that route."*

Finally, there is the ultimate medical excuse - *dying* - and this student didn't let that keep her down - *or* even miss class the next day, according to this memorable story from an anonymous colleague:

- *"I don't know about my worst one (excuse), but I do have the best one... one of my students was late to class one morning because SHE DIED. Literally. She has a congenital heart defect and had to be rushed to the hospital where they revived her during the night. And she still showed up the next morning... just late."*

Chapter 4: The Legal File

In this chapter, we look at how legal issues - run-ins with the law *and* even being detained by the authorities - have made for some very interesting student excuses.

Legal Issues

To begin with, in response to the social media call for best excuses that began the project that became this book, professors readily related their own experiences from their younger years regarding run-ins/close calls with the law:

- *"I forgot to pay a speeding ticket and they arrested me. BTW this is my own excuse from when I was a student!"*

- *"In grad school, I got my own visit from the men in suits (the FBI). A computer I'd set up had been used to attack the CDC. They'd hacked in via my machine, without my knowledge. For a brief moment, several people thought I was a kickass hacker."*

Legals problems - of all types - do cause students to have "issues," as these very real student excuses offered by colleagues from across the country demonstrate:

- *"This is from a number of years ago but still my favorite. Student emailed: 'I was being questioned by the FBI. I can give you the agent's name if you want to check.'"*

- *"A student said he had documentation for his missed classes. He gave me his multiple court summons."*

- *"My university is within 60 kilometers of the American border. Years ago. A student crossed into the closest state and was forbidden by Canadian border guards from returning until some old paperwork from previous protest activities was cleared up. Border guards confirmed the story."*

- *"This is not my story, but from one of my colleagues. He had a student take an exam early because the FBI was looking for him. Sure enough, on the day of the exam, two guys in suits showed up and asked him where the student was."*

And yes, students *do* even get arrested in class - *occasionally*. It can be a show-stopping - well, *lecture-stopping* - moment if it ever does happen to you! I have seen it happen in classes conducted by colleagues, but in over 30 years of teaching, it hasn't happened in my class - yet! But this story shared by a contemporary is a common reaction for those professors who have experienced this phenomenon in one of their classes:

- *"I had a student removed by the police from my class. It was weird. He had an arrest warrant. I was lecturing and police officers came in all three lecture hall doors at the same time. My first thought was, 'What have I done?'"*

And one professor at the University of Virginia even provided a reference for a particularly shocking arrest of one of his students in class:

- "That reminds me, I had one former student hauled off for kidnapping. It was an international news story - see: UVa students' arrests a shock to classmates[1]."

Jail

Unfortunately, college students *do* come into contact with the law - and some do end-up on the wrong side of it. So, being in jail *does* come-up as a reason for being absent, missing a test, or being late on an assignment or project every now and then, as these examples from instructors across America demonstrate:

- *"Miss, I'm sorry I didn't turn in my paper. I was in jail."*

---

1.   https://dailyprogress.com/news/uva-students-arrests-a-shock-to-classmates/
article_4f9d79fa-e228-5037-96c4-ebcacb6cf593.html

- *"My student emailed me saying 'I got caught with weed and spent the weekend as the guest of Fulton County.'"*

- *"I couldn't turn in my paper (extended deadline already, mind you) cos I was in Jail cos my baby daddy called in an amber alert on me."*

- *"One I'll never forget, a student shows up with a massive black eye - 'Sorry I missed class, I was in jail, here's my court paperwork' - no more explanation."*

- *"Student shows up after 2 weeks... 'Sorry professor, I was detained, in Ohio (we are in California) and I need to appear in court again in a week....can I get an extension?'"*

- *"I had one bring me his arrest record as his written documentation for an excuse for missing a quiz."*

- *"I had a student who was sentenced to spend X number of days in jail. Because she was a student, they allowed her to 'spread out' her sentence over numerous months. She missed an exam because she 'had to be in jail.'"*

- *"My favorite reason is still the student who simply told me, 'I was in jail.' And he showed me the bail form thing. I excused it because you can't be in class if you are in jail and a person who's been in jail has enough going on."*

- *"I've had three students miss class because they were incarcerated. Which is hilarious because I've actually said to students, 'Did you miss class because you were in jail?' The last one said, 'As a matter of fact...'" One of this professor's colleagues wisely advised in response, "I learned a long time ago not to go there."*

And then, for the one jail excuse from a colleague that is statistically unlikely, *but* totally true - and worrisome - is this one:

- *"Twelve students in one of my classes missed a test because they were all arrested in the same meth bust."*

Conclusion

Unlike most of the other chapters, this one doesn't conclude with a story of students persevering or overcoming adversity when it comes to legal issues. With the age demographic of traditional college students, issues with the law - some innocent (like parking tickets) *and* some not nearly so innocent - are almost inevitably going to occur with 18-25 year olds. Hopefully though, all of these students - and students in the future - will have learned from these experiences (and maybe even have a great story to tell about them someday!).

However, I will end this chapter with a chilling tale submitted for this project by a colleague from Florida. Unfortunately, these kinds of incidents, though relatively rare thankfully, do really happen, and the thought of such confrontations and threats is a reality for all of us in higher education today.

- *"It's not an especially creative story, but it's one I'll never hard forget! A grad student appeared in my office after flunking several weekly assignments to say that she ALWAYS made A's (her transcript begged to differ) and that she EXPECTED one in this course, too. She indicated a large, heavy handbag and informed me that she always PACKED and she wasn't afraid to use it! The moment she was gone, I was in the Dean's office, of course. They issued a Baker Act for her. That's a Florida Law which permits a 3-day involuntary detention of someone who might be a danger to self or others. She did own guns and had a carry permit and she lived with her brother who was a violent offender. Since she didn't actually pull the gun on me and we couldn't prove she had carried it on campus which is illegal, I had her back in class the next week. She did flunk and it was her last F so she was expelled. I have a bad habit of not locking the doors but—that semester—I locked all the door and tripled checked them."*

Thankfully, her story had a safe ending! But sometimes, such threats and intimidation are indeed real, and it is something that all of us who work in colleges and universities - anywhere in America - do have to be mindful of today.

Chapter 5: The Pets and Animals File

In this chapter, we look at how issues - both real *and* imagined - with the Animal Kingdom have made for some very interesting student excuses.

Animals

Now to begin with, my colleagues from around the country shared experiences from their student days in regards to their own "interesting" animal encounters:

- *"Now mind you, this was before emails through smartphones and laptops that had WiFi. I once was attacked by a dog 20 minutes before class. It happened at my friend's house who I walked to campus with every day. Her mom bandaged me and then drove me to campus so I could walk in to tell my prof that I'd be missing class (that already started) because I had been attacked by a dog. In my defense I had almost passed out and was out of it. He looked at me strangely and shrugged his shoulders and went on teaching. I almost passed out walking out of class."*

- *"I live and work in metro Boston; the wild turkey is a protected species in Massachusetts. If you touch a turkey, you can be fined. In a grad school class, I was once 15 minutes late to a group meeting to work on our final project because a group of turkeys had wandered into the road. All the cars were stuck in place until the turkeys decided to meander to one side of the road or the other."*

- *"Had a student be late because she said that there was a sea turtle crossing the road. (she lived in Tybee island and taught at Georgia Southern, so this is a legit thing there)." To which a fellow animal loving colleague replied: "One day after a big storm, I had to stop to help about a dozen turtles across the road on my drive into town (I live in rural Kentucky). I was late for my 8:30 am meeting by about 10 minutes. Everyone agreed I did the right thing."*

My contemporaries' reports of student encounters with animals of *all* types were - without a doubt - "interesting" as well, and represented many different parts of the Animal Kingdom!:

- *"One of mine got bitten by a duck."*

- *"We have a large equine program on our campus so about once a year a horse dies. Student emails me: 'Sorry I will not be in class professor but I had to attend a necropsy and I'm covered in blood.' I said 'You go change, kid!' (we get a list of students attending-she was legit)."*

- *"Ok this one was actually true, though it sounds fake. A student called me (knowing I'd never believe an email) that she couldn't get out of her house to come to class because there was a mountain lion on her porch! (It's Colorado, so this stuff happens haha)...Similarly, I had a colleague get stuck in his house when a family of skunks moved in under his porch!"*

- *"I had a student whose 20+ goats got out of their pen. Someone a few miles away called the sheriff when she saw a tribe of goats wandering down her dirt road. She sent me this beautiful picture of when they found the goats on a tree lined road in the country. It took hours to round them up and get them home."*

- *"I had a student miss the final exam because she was 'mauled by a bear.' True story - it was big news in my neck of the woods! P.S. She was okay. But that's <u>exactly</u> how she worded the email."*

- *"Student was late because she said she ran over an otter on the way to class. then proceeded to pull out her phone and show me photos of the deceased. I've never heard anything so unusual in my life. 'Otterly' unbelievable! It was better than the student that told me they slipped and fell in the shower then self diagnosed they sustained a concussion and couldn't make it."*

- *"A student missed a test after a run-in with a bat necessitated rabies shots."*

- *"Student emailed me to the effect: 'I raise hairless guinea pigs and we just had babies. The mother rejected them and I have to feed them every two hours around the clock. I can't find someone to cover the shift during your final exam. Could I take it another time?' I shit you not.' Puppies I get. Hairless guinea pigs? I didn't even know that was a thing! Then I saw a photo on Facebook years later and was amazed. This was the last excuse of the year. She literally had an excuse every single test for all three quarters. I promised myself I would not excuse her for any reason. This took the cake!"*

- *"Yesterday while we were in a Zoom class, one of my students got a bat in her room and we all watched (transfixed and yelling encouragement) while her apartment maintenance dude ran around with a bag and a ladder trying to catch it."*

Now, cows seem to be a category all their own when it comes to causing student "issues":

- *"I had a student that said she needed to miss class for the birth of a calf at home. I confirmed she did actually live on a farm. She also volunteered to give me pics of the occasion. I told her...that's okay, just come to the next class. Lol"*

- *"Student called right before class...My cow is birthing a calf and it is breech so I have to assist. Definitely gave a pass on that one."*

- *"A young woman in my Western Civ course came up to explain that she would miss class a couple of weeks into the fall semester because she had qualified to exhibit her champion Holstein at the state fair. A) She was shocked that I didn't freak out, but I am from this area so I get it; And B) For farm families, the purse and sale of the state champion means a lot of money for the winner. I wished her luck, and by gum, they won!"*

- *"I teach in a rural area and one of my best students apologized profusely when telling me that he couldn't make it to class because 'the cows got out and they were roaming onto the county road' and he had to go round them up. I am sure it was true and it was the only class he missed the entire time he was my student (in multiple courses)."*

Finally, there are those animal encounters that students have that end up being *really* serious for students - in their real lives well beyond the classroom:

- *"Well... I actually believed my student because I had mostly rural students. He called me over in the middle of lecture and was like. 'Um, Prof., Can I leave because my gf just got bit by a water moccasin (poisonous snake) in the back yard and she's home alone? We have called an exterminator but I guess they missed one.' Later when he wasn't coming to class I emailed him to see if they were ok. He apologized and said he couldn't do class anymore because she was a hairdresser and got bit on the hand so they had to watch it to see whether she would have to amputate... in the meantime he would have to be the sole income."*

Pets

Pets bring such joy to our lives, and we all have experienced pets being sick, lost, or other concerns. Perhaps pet-related excuses are so powerful (i.e. they work!) because we can *all* relate to them! And yes, many student excuses stem from our dogs, our cats, and yes, our ferrets:

- *"My student missed class from taking his puppy to the vet after the dog began to act weird from getting into a stash of weed. So crazy that is not on the list of excusable absences."*

- *"I had a student who missed the first several weeks of class and several assignments and said it was because their cat had been sick."*

- *"Student's puppy had eaten a 3" screw. She legit emailed me the x-rays from the vet."*

- *"One student said her cat got caught in the dishwasher..." (And no, this professor didn't say if the story had a happy or sad ending...)*

- *"One of my students: 'Sorry I had to leave the meeting early. My dog licked my eye.' I laughed, told her I'd never heard that one before, and reminded her to finish her work."*

- *"Lost her ferret in the vent..."*

- *"I had a student once meet me outside the classroom prior to the final exam to inform me she wasn't staying to take it. She explained that she had an asthmatic cat at home and she was worried that she had forgotten to turn on the air conditioner. I was an adjunct at the time, and she created a major hoopla when she received a zero on it."*

And yet, pet stories can be *absolutely* true - and yes, it *really* helps of you're a student with credibility telling it!:

- "A cat was stuck in our air vent and we had to rescue it. Here's a picture of the cat as proof. (This is one of the kindest hearted students I have ever had, and I have had her for several classes. I definitely believed her.)"

But then there are students that have fake pets, much like fake aunts, grandmothers, and close friends. Below is the best story on this point from a contemporary:

- "Student emailed me saying, 'My dog was hit by a car and I had to take him for emergency surgery.' I got a colleague to ask him how his dog was doing. He replied, 'Dog?'"

Conclusion

Now while we may laugh at some of these pet and animal-related excuses for their statistical unlikelihood and their absurdity, we all know that there are also excuses in this realm that are *both* absolutely true and in many cases, positively inspiring.

First, we have an excuse submitted by one of my fellow college faculty members where the professor regretted how he handled the situation. In fact, this one anonymous colleague felt bad - *really bad* - about the consequences of what happened to one of his students' pets, partially on his account:

- "A few years ago I lectured my students about how important it was for them to come to class. Then I had a student whose dog ran away and who stopped looking for him to come to class. I felt horrible."

And then we have a story from another contemporary that is almost beyond belief. In this case, the student was not just very fortunate to survive her animal encounter, but came back to class way faster than most any other human could after what she had survived:

- "I had a student that was riding a horse over an 8 foot high footbridge and she fell off the horse to the ground below the footbridge and then the horse fell on top of her. It broke both of her legs and one arm, but she came back to class three days later."

Chapter 6: The Weather File

In this chapter, we look at how weather issues - and students' perceptions of the weather - can come into play in "interesting" ways as rain, sleet, snow, and yes, *even wind*, have made for some very interesting student excuses.

Weather Issues

While we may have had to walk uphill through the snow and rain to go to class (I actually had one contemporary proudly say, *"I used to walk 1.3 miles to class in upstate NY year around, rain, snow, or shine. I get a kick out of laughing at student excuses about the weather!"*), weather is a common source of students trying to excuse their absences or late work today. And while the postman would do his (or her) job based on the U.S. Postal Service's[1] famous motto: *"Neither snow nor rain nor heat nor gloom of night stays these couriers from the swift completion of their appointed rounds,"* that is not necessarily how students - well, *some* students - approach weather concerns today. Consider these weather-related excuses submitted by my contemporaries from around the country:

- *"We had a student say that she missed class because it was too windy!!!"*

- *"When I taught in Los Angeles I would regularly get 'it's raining!' as an excuse for not coming to class."*

- *"I had a student email me that he stepped in a puddle on the way to class and got his sock all wet, so wouldn't be able to make it..."*

Now certainly, weather causes especially dicey issues for students, as one person's perception of "serious" is *far* different than another's in many cases. But to some college students, *"Baby, it's cold outside"*

---

1. https://www.usps.com/

is more than just a song! Winter weather seems to be especially troublesome for students to deal with - in a variety of ways:

- *"Years ago, a student emailed me to let me know they'd be absent because their car windshield had ice on it and they lost their snow brush. It snowed less than an inch the night before. In NE Ohio!"*

- *"A student just told me he couldn't Zoom class because his car was stuck in the driveway due to snow. He has the internet at home and a laptop."*

- *"Best excuse: 'I am not from here and the weather has been too cold for me to come to class.' (Note: We had a mild fall that year, lots of sun, and, regardless, his dorm was connected to the building by UNDERGROUND TUNNELS so he would not have to experience the weather in the first place)."*

- *"I had a student once call to tell me he missed class because he was snowed in an hour away. This was in the days before everyone had cell phones. Caller ID told me he was calling from his dorm room!"*

However, other faculty responded with info on how much tougher they and their students were, based on their local climate. Now this kind of "weather trash talk" puts us Sunbelt and Southern folks in our place! In fact, two of my New Orleans' colleagues responded with circumstances unique to areas like ours in the South:

- *"I can remember our school closing just because it went below 32 degrees and they were afraid pipes would freeze and what would we do if a fire broke out???"*

- *"In New Orleans that would happen with the slightest dusting of snow. It's so rare that we'd ALL probably stop class to go experience it."*

So yes, there are some areas of the country where winter weather has to be *extreme* to shut things down!:

- From a faculty member in Kansas City, Missouri:

"It has been below -6 here, and it has to be below zero for them to close schools for the cold."

- From a faculty member in Bancroft, Idaho:

"It has to be -20 here for schools to close."

So, in the end, unless it is an "automatic" - where a blizzard, a hurricane, or the aftereffects of severe storms causes schools, and often everything in an area to shut down - students and faculty members have to use their own judgement as to when weather should keep one from classes. And different universities take very different approaches to closing for weather concerns, with some hardly ever doing so and some doing so at the veritable "drop of a hat" (or *rain* as the case may be!). At my own university however, which has a high percentage of commuter students, weather concerns *do* pose a special concern. And while over the years there have been times where we've been open when no one could believe that we were due to weather concerns and vice versa, to a person, I have found my colleagues to generally give students the "benefit of the doubt" - and *especially so* for commuting students - and accede to their issues with driving to campus under severe weather conditions.

And speaking of perceptions, one faculty member pointed out how cultural differences can come into play when considering weather issues. She reported becoming enlightened herself about how weather can indeed impact people from different cultures in very different ways from just such a student encounter:

- "Ok so the rain thing. I've had it happen a few times. After unpacking it....one of my African American girls just straight up said I don't come in downpours. —-it has more to do with the cost it would take to fix her hair if it got that wet. I never thought of it and the pressure for Black women and hair I can only imagine."

Conclusion

Now while we may laugh at some of these weather-related excuses for their statistical unlikelihood and their absurdity, we all know that there are also excuses in this realm that are *both* absolutely true and in many cases, positively inspiring.

Lest one think all weather-related excuses are made-up (or over-exaggerated, at least) by students, "STUFF" *does* happen - and yes, professors do prove what those of us in academia know. This is the fact that by and large, college faculty are a very understanding *and* empathetic group of individuals, as shown by this story - involving the proverbial "tree that fell on the student's house!" (something that *yes*, happened to my own son in college!) - and my colleague's very understanding reaction to the student's "tree problem":

- *"Ummmm. A student said that they had to stop taking their midterm because a tree fell on their house during a storm. They included a picture of themselves standing by a tree that had blown into their home, caving in the roof. I allowed them to reschedule."*

Chapter 7: The Home File

In this chapter, we look at how issues at home - from home maintenance and repairs to yes, *bugs*, and roommate problems - have made for some very interesting student excuses.

Home Issues

Ah, we all know how our college apartments and rent houses were things that we might fondly - *or not so fondly* - remember. The same is true for today's students, as home issues seem to be a common cause of attendance issues. This is exemplified by the following excuses, submitted by anonymous colleagues from universities all across America.

First, there are just the "things" that happen around the house, like these - especially around test times!:

- *"Student said her power went out and she had no idea how to open the garage since the button wasn't working."*

- *"I had a student who opened the cabinets in her kitchen, and a baking sheet fell out and hit her on the head! The student was fine, just wanted to take the test later!"*

And then there are the excuses related to plumbing problems - and yes, most of these have to deal with "toilet issues" - so be warned!:

- *"I received a photo of an overflowing toilet. I believe you. You don't have to send me that."*

- *"I had a student flush homemade ramen with jumbo shrimp and it flooded their room and soaked their clothes and bag so they couldn't go to class. Yes, I received photos..."*

- *"I had a student refuse to come to class due to not being able to get a shower for that day. I guess repairs were being made."* To which another professor replied: *"I wish some of mine did that! I've had way too many come to class smelling like the previous night's party."*

- *"I had a student who missed class because he locked himself INSIDE his own room. It needed a key to get out and he had to wait for his mom to get home to let him out. He even had his mom call me to tell me and take a picture of the door. He was a great student I knew well, so I didn't even doubt him."*

And of course, then there are *bugs...*

- *"When I was an undergrad, I woke up to go to class and discovered an Indian meal moth (aka 'pantry moth') larvae infestation in the closet of my dorm room. (which also served as part pantry). Emailed my prof right away that I would be missing class to deal with it. I was worried it wouldn't be counted as an excused absence because it seemed so absurd. Later, my professor said she knew I was telling the truth because it was the wildest reason for missing class she'd ever heard. It was one of the worst days of my life, though. So disgusting!"*

- *"A colleague had a student ask for an extension to an assignment because there was a moth infestation at her house and she couldn't work because there were moths attacking her and her computer screen."*

- *"'My roommates and I have lice!'...it was true, but definitely a first. She later sent me photos of all them in different stages of lice treatment!"*

There are some home issues that are no doubt *very* serious, such as this one, which proves that unfortunately, sometimes "STUFF" *does* happen:

- *"I received a pic of a fireman holding a hose outside an apartment building from a student, followed by an email explaining that it was a real time pic of her home! All ended well—no injuries or significant damage!"*

And then there are the roommate issues...

- *"Had a student say he was late because his roommate used his bar of soap and filled it with hair, rendering it useless for him to shower with..."*

- *"Student related that he couldn't come to class 'because the water in the dorm was turned off and he couldn't shower or brush his teeth.' To which I shared my stories of being embedded with the Marines during the Battle of Fallujah."*

- "A student told me today that he missed Wednesday's class because his roommates asked him to 'hit it' and he forgot to come to class. I think he just told me he missed class to get high."

- "I always appreciate an excuse from a student that I haven't heard before because they are so crazy they have to be true. I once had a student borrow a Post-It Note poster pad for a class presentation. He came to me later and confessed that he could not return it because his roommate had been drinking and when my student suggested slowing down, the roommate sped up in protest, got sick, and puked all over it. He didn't think I would want it back (which I agreed!) and he offered to buy me a new one. I told him that the story alone was worth the replacement cost!"

Conclusion

Unlike most of the other chapters, this one doesn't conclude with a story of students persevering or overcoming adversity when it comes to home issues. Hopefully though, all of these students - and students in the future - will have learned from these experiences (and maybe even have a great story to tell about them someday!). And yes, we can all hope that they find better places to live - *and* in some cases, better folks to share their homes with - in their future lives.

Chapter 8: The Family File

In this chapter, we look at how family issues - both real *and* imagined - come into play with kids, spouses, and yes, even grandpa, making for some very interesting student excuses today.

Family Issues

Colleagues around the country who contributed their best student excuses sometimes offered ones from their own experiences regarding family issues and how their professors handled such events when they occurred, including this one that shows just how much all of us remember those professors who are understanding of family issues when they inevitably do arise:

- *"Personally, I missed a final exam during my PhD coursework because I was sitting in the hospital with my husband after he came out from surgery. I told him I might be late to the exam. He told me to stay at the hospital. He was the best!"*

From the responses garnered from my contemporaries in higher education, just as I have experienced in my own teaching career, family issues have been a common area for student excuses. Such excuses include items like:

- *"One student told me she missed class because she got in a fight with her sister and had to keep ice on her eye."*

- *"My favorite was 'I have to go turkey hunting with my Dad'—I gave him the extension he requested."*

- *"I had a student miss a midterm exam because his mom told him to babysit his sisters."*

- *"Had to go house hunting with his parents."*

- *"This was before remote instruction but I had a student say they had to miss class b/c they had to help the family with their garage sale. When I said that would be an absence, they asked if I would Skype them in [while they helped at the sale].*"

And yes, this one is my personal favorite - perhaps of *any* of the hundreds of excuses submitted to me by my colleagues for this project:

- "*Student said: 'I couldn't finish my essay last night because I had to go bail Grandpa out of jail.' And it turned out to be true.*"

Sometimes though, one can encounter a family-related student excuse that can leave you concerned - *and* worried!:

- "*One of my favorites, from a non-trad student in class that met at night just once a week: 'I had to miss class because my daughter just got her very first period and I needed to stay home to snuggle with her.' I was conflicted about how to respond to that one!*"

Then again, there are family issues that make us appreciate just how different cultures are around the world:

- "*Student told me: 'My father has been kidnapped by Tamil rebels in Sri Lanka.' Two days later, asked him if he had word about his father. 'Yes, Madam, I spoke to him last night.' I replied, 'But you said he had been kidnapped?' She responded: 'O Madam, you are not understanding how things are in my country. He is kidnapped, but we are talking.'*"

Conclusion

Now while we may laugh at some of these family-related excuses for their statistical unlikelihood and their absurdity, we all know that there are also excuses in this realm that are *both* absolutely true and in many cases, positively inspiring.

Yes, there are so many situations where family causes students not to go awry, but to go above and beyond, like this story from a fellow professor:

- "*Had a mother and daughter in the same class. Mom shows up, takes me aside, and says, 'My daughter hit black ice and tore out a barbed wire fence on the way here, flipped the car, and is in the ER.' I told her: 'Please go back to the hospital.' It messed the daughter's back up pretty badly and she ended up withdrawing. This was before widespread cellular use, so her mother came all the way to campus to tell me."*

And sometimes, you just have to marvel at how students, particularly adult students with very real *and* very serious family concerns, pull things together to still do well in school, no matter what might be going on in their "real" lives:

- *"I had a student who emailed me in August, just before classes started. She informed me that she was taking the class from St. Jude because her daughter (3 years old) was getting cancer treatments. I had the syllabus out with exam dates. She asked if there was any way possible to take the exam, scheduled in October, early because the Make A Wish foundation scheduled a Disney trip the week of the exam. This student never turned a single assignment in late."*

Chapter 9: The Social File (Including Alcohol)

In this chapter, we look at how social issues - both real *and* imagined - come into play, and see how friends - *and* friends with alcohol, particularly those in fraternities and sororities, of course - and can make for some very interesting student excuses today.

Social Excuses

Ah, the things we do and learn about in college *outside* of the classroom! We know that students learn so much from the extracurricular side of college, both from the formal, school-sponsored and/or approved activities, but even more so in most cases, from the other aspects of life outside the classroom. And so, in this chapter, we will explore three areas of the social aspects of college life
1. Social Life
2. Greek Life
3. Partying (Yes, with Alcohol!)

Social Life

There are such a wide range of social reasons that can come into play with college students, and as faculty, we can *and* do empathize with such issues. From an anonymous contemporary came a remembrance of her own college days in Idaho - at an event that yes, you would indeed not likely find in *any* of the other 49 states:

- *"I missed class once because the campus hosted a mash potato slip n slide (in Idaho), as I stood up I rolled my foot on a ping-pong ball and twisted my ankle. However the ping-pong ball did have the winning number for a boom box. So at least I got a prize too."*

And living and teaching just outside of New Orleans, there are excuses we see on occasion that are unique to our area, such as:

- *"More than one student informed me she had to miss a week of classes to prepare for her cotillion."*

- *"I can't come to class because I'm a queen on a Mardi Gras float. Attached is a letter from the director of the parade excusing my absence."*

I personally cannot tell you how many Mardi Gras-related excuses I have fielded over almost thirty years of teaching in this area - and yes, some have involved students who honestly had partied a bit too hard at Mardi Gras to be back in class on Ash Wednesday or later that week.

And what is college without the friendships and relationships we build along the way, and yes, these can be the source of some "interesting" excuses to say the least!:

- *"A student asked me a week in advance if they could skip lab to 'pregame for the football game.' I replied: 'No buddy, you can't without penalty!'"*

- *"My student missed a test because his pal needed a ride from the airport."*

Romantic relationships are a source of excuses that have some students providing *way too much* information in the hopes of getting an absence excused or a shot at a make-up test:

- *"My girlfriend has her period and I had to stay home to comfort her."*

- *"A student emailed me that she couldn't come to class because she and her boyfriend 'were having too much sex and she got a UTI and now the antibiotics were giving her diarrhea.' Still my favorite ever!"*

- *"Student missed an exam and I saw him in the hallway later that day. When asked about his absence, he replied: 'I was in the middle of a threesome.'"*

Greek Life

Fraternity and sorority activities - and the aftermath of them - seemed to be a common cause of students' absences or missing deadlines. And perhaps surprisingly to some, students can be quite honest - sometimes *too honest* - about how Greek life impacted their schoolwork.

- *"Student asked for an extension on a paper because they wanted to wait until they were sober to write it. It was over a fraternity initiation weekend."*

- *"I became unexpectedly ill after a fraternity event."* (To which the professor added that he *"gave the student points for honesty!"*).

- *"A student emailed me from his fraternity telling me he was sick. It was Greek Row week and he was outside all day building the fence around their yard for it. Their frat house was directly across the street from the office windows in our building. I had been watching him build it and drink beer all day. I emailed him back 'I see you, you're drinking beer.' That was it!"*

- *"I will be too drunk to come to class on Monday after initiation."*

- *"I had a student who couldn't come to class because he was in the middle of a frat war and someone lit his porch on fire."*

Partying (Yes, with Alcohol!)

Alcohol is undoubtedly part of the college experience for many, many students. And while the dangers of drinking - and particularly both alcoholism and binge drinking - are to be taken *extremely seriously*, that is not our purpose here. In this section, we will review the alcohol-related excuses shared by professors from all over the country.

Alcohol can indeed lead to some incredible - *but true* - student excuses:

- *"I had one email that he missed class because the night before he got drunk, tried to jump a fence, and broke his face. He then attached a picture of his bruised and bloody face."*

- *"I was in an evening class (as a student) when another student's (Let's call her Kathy) phone rang. She picks up. Caller was another student from the same class (who was usually attending class faithfully). Let's call him Joe. After the call, Kathy raises her hand to let the teacher know that Joe won't make it to class, because he is currently in a bar and has had too much to drink."*

- "I had a student once tell me she couldn't show up for our exam because her son's birthday party had gotten out of hand and she was still hung over."

And with 21 being the legal drinking age in almost every instance, 21st birthdays seem to be a common source of alcohol-related excuses:

- "I had a student tell me in advance she was going to be absent because she would be hungover - two days later. 21st birthday... at least she had a solid plan?"

- "A student, who I knew had not come to class yet during the semester (I didn't grade attendance but still took it at the time), emailed that they wouldn't be there to turn in a project in person because it had been their best friends 21st birthday the day before and she was still too hungover to come to class."

- "I had 3 students ask for an excused absence to go to a baseball game. 2 wanted to get the 3rd drunk for his 21st birthday instead of coming to class."

Conclusion

Now while we may laugh at some of these social-related excuses for their statistical unlikelihood and their absurdity, we all know that there are also excuses in this realm that are *both* absolutely true and in many cases, positively inspiring.

Yes, sometimes faculty members have to deal with students who present social and relationship issues that are *very* serious and call upon them to use their people skills to the hilt:

- "I had a student miss a lot of assignments because his girlfriend was pregnant. He said he was stressed with being a father at a very young age."

Unfortunately today, the very "real world" problems with crime and violence *do* impact our students, as this colleague's story - and the context he provides to this one very dedicated student's story - shows:

- *"I once had a student come to my office and apologize for missing a day of our class. His apartment had just been robbed while he was in it, and he said he would have come to class but he had been hit on the head with a pistol grip and needed a few stitches. He was back by the next class and kept working his way through the course, which was a math course for future elementary and middle school teachers. Unfortunately, it was not the last time a student of mine encountered a robbery, but I do believe it's the only armed robbery with the student present that I've had come up."*

And this one excuse story is certainly a positive note to end on with the honesty shown by this student as it pertains to alcohol use (or misuse):

- *"I had a student come apologize for missing the previous class. They looked me right in the eye and said, 'I turned 21 the night before and I was so hungover. The shape I was in, my presence would have been a disrespect to you and your class.' They were clear they weren't trying to get the absence excused. They believed in always telling the truth, but wanted to be clear they took the class seriously. I will never forget that unabashed, yet entirely respectful honesty."*

Chapter 10: The Technology File

In this chapter, we look at how technology issues - both real *and* imagined - come into play for students, and how modern technology, *or the lack thereof*, can be a very modern problem - *and* excuse - for college students today.

Technology Problems

To begin with, this one might be my fave out of all the tech-related excuses offered by my contemporaries on this front, one of whom recounted a very real encounter with one of her students:

- *"Student: 'I'm so sorry I've fallen behind, I'm homeless and it's been really hard. I haven't been able to talk to my friends or family for a while now.'*

Me: Cue my instant empathy, I start asking questions about her having a safe place to sleep and offer suggestions to help with potential food insecurity

Student (indignant): 'I didn't say I was HOMEless, I said I was PHONEless. I lost my phone last week and it sucks cause I can't talk to anyone.'

Me: Wow!"

There were certainly a wide range of tech issues that students encountered - *or* at least said they encountered - and tried to use as excuses with their professors:

- *"Once a student said her mouse froze on the screen so she couldn't do any work for a week."*

- *"Some variation of the water + technology problem happens every semester, but my favorite was: 'Sorry I couldn't upload my presentation because I dropped my phone in the toilet while I was playing Pokemon Go and that caused the upload to stop and now I don't have a phone.'"*

Students also reported very "first world" problems when it came to technology issues:

- *"I once had a student miss the midterm. It was online and available for 2 days. A week later he came to me and asked to make it up. I said no. He said he was on a ski trip and there was bad wifi/reception. I still said no. He said he owns a successful IT business and could pay me. The look of horror on my face... his friend pulled his arm and said 'time to go, man.'"*

And yes, professors can turn the tables on students when it comes to technology:

- *"I used to have students that would say 'I have an important call, I have to go.' I have no idea why, but I would say 'I don't care if it's baby Jesus... you can't answer it and sit down.' One day, a student said... 'OMG, I have a call coming in and I have to take it... you will never guess who it is... BABY JESUS!' Sure enough, the caller ID said 'Baby Jesus.' We answered the call as a class, and it was the best phone call ever!"*

- *"I remember the time I took a student's phone away from him because he was texting a girl? I texted her from his phone and asked her out for him! They dated for awhile!"*

- *"I had a student turn in a paper on the civil rights movement printed in yellow ink because 'his printer ran out of every other color.' Turns out he must've been channeling Dr. Martin Luther King Jr. as he wrote the paper because it was the Doctor's words, so eloquently, though barely visibly, printed on those pages!"*

Today, there also seems to be a trend at the intersection of technology and the Animal Kingdom:

- *"I had a student seriously tell me she lost her homework on her computer because — wait for it — a raccoon came in through an open window and ate the wires on her computer thus making it useless and she couldn't get it fixed in time to hand it her work. I asked for pictures of the destruction to the apartment she claimed but somehow never saw them. That's my best story."*

- "I had a student tell me that their puppy ate the flash drive with all their work on it. An updated version of 'the dog ate my homework!'" To which one of her fellow professors commented, "Funny, but we had a dog that ate MY flash drive."

Conclusion

Now while we may laugh at some of these tech-related excuses for their statistical unlikelihood and their absurdity, we all know that there are also excuses in this realm that are *both* absolutely true and in many cases, positively inspiring.

And so in dealing with such issues, sometimes students will show a great deal of perseverance in overcoming their technology problems:

- "One of my legitimately awesome students emailed me at the end of the semester to say she wasn't sure she'd get her work in on time. The day before, she had been in a hurry to get her kids to daycare before she had to be at work and left her laptop with all her final term papers and projects on it in a taxi cab. I gave her an extension, but she was a superstar and still got her work completed on time (and accidentally sent me one of her finals for another class as well, so I know she was working hard!)."

- "Last summer, an active duty student enrolled in my course while deployed 'over there.' His work was hit and miss in terms of punctuality; He let me know up front he probably should not have enrolled while deployed. He messaged me one week that he hadn't been able to do his work because he had to be 'outside the wire' (military terminology for attacking the enemy) with no communication. He finished the course with an extension: very respectful and hard-working when he could. His internet connection was in a tent/mess hall the whole time, so not exactly an ideal environment."

Chapter 11: The Car File

In this chapter, we look at how car issues - both real *and* imagined - and yes, some that *are* deadly serious, have served as excuses for college students today.

Car Problems

To begin with, while we may laugh at some of the car-related student excuses reported by my contemporaries from across the country, some can - *and* are - life-threatening situations. To illustrate this fact, let's begin with a story related by an anonymous colleague from a much colder climate than my own. He responded to my call for student excuses with a car-related story from his own college days - and he was indeed lucky to be alive to do so:

- *"This is my own story. As an undergrad, I got hit by my own car after putting the car in park to retrieve mail from the mailbox. Car slipped into reverse, so I chased it down. I got hit by the door twice when trying to jump into the moving vehicle. Knocked me down and then hit me in the head when I bounced up. No worries though, just a concussion and I was able to jump up again to stop my car before it made it to my grandma's in-ground pool. My professor's mouth gaped wide open as I told the story."*

Now students have used car-related excuses that span the gamut from comical to deadly serious (and yes, sometimes they have been known to lie about their car issues):

- *"I once had a student tell me she was so exhausted from car shopping all day that she could not take the final exam."*

- *"Years ago, a student emailed me to let me know they'd be absent because their car windshield had ice on it and they lost their snow brush. It snowed less than an inch the night before. In NE Ohio!"*

- *"Student sent an email about his absence: '..Not my fault! My car was towed (with my blue book inside) because I accidentally left it in a 'no parking' zone when I was doing the responsible thing by NOT driving home drunk the night before.'"*

Car Accidents and Incidents

Car accidents are an unfortunate - *and* serious - matter, but sometimes students may try to make-up a car wreck excuse...

- *"A colleague's student notified them that they'd been in a car accident. They sent photos as proof. The colleague thought the photos looked weird and just Googled 'car wreck' on a whim, and the student's 'proof' were the first photos that came up in the search."*

Sadly of course, many times, the accidents *are* all too real...

- *"Final exam, in-person. At the start of the period about 2/3 of the students I expected were there... the rest dribbled in over about 10 minutes, noting there was a car accident blocking traffic. The last student came in and told me about the car accident he'd just been in on the way into campus."*

- *"I will say I once had a student apologize for being late to class. He waited until after he turned in his midterm to tell me he'd been in a car accident and was trying to find a doctor's appointment for after my class. I begged him to please email me after he'd been to urgent care. He did *not* look okay."*

And yes, sometimes the truth about the accident - or *accidents* - is stranger than any fiction one could write:

- *"Had a student miss class because he hit a deer on the way to campus. Missed the next class because he needed to get a rental car, having totaled his by hitting the deer, and had to find someone to rent it for him because he was under 25. Missed the third class because he hit a deer in the rental. All documented. All true. Told him he should buy an orange car moving forward."*

Finally, sadly in the age in which we live, students sometimes find themselves being car theft/carjacking victims, and such stories can be truly horrifying:

- "A student once told me they could not submit their final project, as their car had been stolen that morning while at the gas station. The next day they arrived with a police report and photos of the burned car with the charred project visible in the trunk. Yup - excuse accepted!"

- "Student missed a stats exam because they had recently been carjacked and forced at gunpoint to drive around to different ATMs and empty their bank accounts, at the end of which and for good measure they took their car containing their notes and stats book. Confirmed with police investigating the case."

Conclusion

Now while we may laugh at some of these automobile-related excuses for their statistical unlikelihood and their absurdity, we all know that there are also excuses in this realm that are *both* absolutely true and in many cases, positively inspiring.

And so in dealing with such car issues, here's a final excuse submitted by a colleague that exemplifies how some students will persevere, no matter their circumstances:

- "One semester, I had only one student in a class that had a job off campus. Although this student lived on campus, they commuted 25 minutes twice a day, in the morning for a few hours before class and again after. One day this student learned how to change a flat tire, on the side of the interstate, from watching YouTube... and still made it to class. They walked in about halfway through, quietly took a seat, and engaged in class without any sort of disruption."

Chapter 12: The Food and Drink File

In this chapter, we look at how issues - both real *and* imagined - with foods of all types and beverages of all sorts (but usually coffee!) can make for some very interesting student excuses today.

Food and Drink Issues

To begin with, all of us on faculty today likely have memories of how food and drink issues came into play in our own college experience, including some involving our own professors, such as this one submitted anonymously by a colleague:

- *"Can we count excuses for former professors? I had an undergrad professor show up late to class (as usual) and tell us that he was sorry he was late. He would have been on time except he knew we expected him to be late, so he stopped to eat a bagel. I will say that although the lateness was frustrating, he was still overall a great prof."*

When it comes to being late for class or for a test because of food and drink issues today, Starbucks seems to be the leading cause of student tardiness today! This is evidenced by the following comment from a fellow faculty member:

- *"A student walks in late with a Starbucks cup. 'The line was soooo long!'" To which a fellow professor responded: "Ugh! I had a student do this Every. Single. Day. Normally, I do everything to ensure a student doesn't fail, but I loved giving her the F she totally deserved!"*

Now some students, likely with a high degree of emotional intelligence, thought that buying their professor a cup of coffee would be the way to get their lateness/absence excused - and they were right in these instances!:

- *"I once got an email from Starbucks: 'What would you like to drink?' How much can you complain when the late students bring you a treat along the way?"*

- "I had a student bring me a drink to soften the blow of being late. No regrets."

The food and drink-related excuses submitted by my contemporaries from all over the country were, to say the least, *interesting*:

- "Student (who always wanted extra credit) packed up and got up to leave 40 min into the class. 'What's up?' I asked. 'It's free pancake day at IHOP!'"

- "I had a student who said he was late to class because he was eating a waffle."

- "I ate too much Halloween candy."

- "Student emailed me that 'he couldn't come to class because of allergic reaction to pumpkin beer.'"

Gastrointestinal Issues from Eating the Wrong Thing

As we discussed in the medical excuses chapter earlier, students will *always* use stomach issues as a "go to" excuse - and detail the food that caused it (and many will provide *way too much* information on what caused them to get sick!):

- "In grad school, my first professor specifically told students not to eat convenience store hot dogs on exam day. Grad school, public health... Students should have figured this out on their own."

- "Student missed an in-person exam due to eating a bad burrito. Unfortunately, they provided GRAPHIC detail about the digestive consequences of said burrito."

- "One semester, a recurring excuse was a digestive malady that students believed to be brought on by a dining hall called 'Observatory Hill' or 'O'Hill' for short. Try to guess the students' name for the malady. Yep, 'O'Bola.' (There was a complete scrubdown of the facility and it was

*eventually determined that norovirus was the culprit... *not* people in the dining hall putting soap in the food!)."*

- "My Japanese students have been known to tell me they were suffering from 'sushi bowels.'"

But when you try to play the "gastro card," students would be well-advised to get their story - *and* their technology - in line:

- "Student emailed me 'I will miss class due to food poisoning.' Then, a second email came from with a photo of her using a beer bong labeled 'check out last night, Carmen.' Then a third email came, frantically telling me not to open the second because she sent it to a friend with the same first name. I sent back an email stating only 'unexcused absence' (although I did think for a min that this really is a sort of food poisoning)."

Conclusion

Unlike most of the other chapters, this one doesn't conclude with a story of students persevering or overcoming adversity when it comes to food and drink issues. Hopefully though, all of these students - and students in the future - will have learned from these experiences (and maybe even have a great story to tell about them someday!).

Chapter 13: The Online Classes/Zoom File

In this chapter, we look specifically at how issues arise in online/Zoom classes and how "real world" issues can impinge - *or* even make impossible - one's ability to engage in learning in the online environment, making for some very interesting student excuses today.

Online Classes and Zoom-Related Excuses

This book is being written in the time of the COVID-19 pandemic[1], an event that has changed so very many aspects of our daily lives. And certainly, the coronavirus outbreak has caused a massive shift in the world of higher education, with more classes being taught online than ever before. Suddenly, even the most tech averse professors were teaching online, and platforms like Zoom, Google Meet, and Webex became lifelines for enabling classes and learning to carry on in spite of the dangers of the virus. And of course, with a rush to online classes, that meant that there would be a rush of excuses for online classes as well! These will be explored here.

To begin, it's not just students who have "issues" with online classes. Indeed, sometimes it is the instructor who makes the mistake about where to be online on their calendar for the day:

- "I was 30 minutes late to a Zoom lab meeting because I was sitting in the wrong zoom session. I was really pissed that not one student showed up. I was really sheepish when I went to the right zoom. They were all there waiting for me."

And this - being in the wrong virtual place - is now a common issue today, even for professors:

---

1. https://www.cdc.gov/coronavirus/2019-nCoV/index.html

- *"I've done that. I was only about 15 minutes late. I only knew because a student texted me to ask if we were still having class. 'Yeah! I'm waiting!'"*

- *"If that happens after about a few minutes I realize that I'm the problem and that's the first thing I check!"*

- *"I did this last semester... after emailing them all to ask them where they were and they replied 'um, in the Live Lecture session?' I apologized profusely, gave them all a 'one unexcused absence no penalty' day at any point in the semester as my thanks for not making fun of me too much."*

Sometimes, the offline and online worlds do collide in interesting ways for all of us:

- *"Today's version of why I'm late is from a colleague. It's COVID and therefore virtual. Her school is mandating a fire drill so she had to push back our meeting. .... while it is legitimate, why on earth does the school have a fire drill virtually?"*

- *"Ok so I had to miss my history class this past semester and asked to zoom into it because I started an experiment for my research and in an instance of poor planning, the reaction was longer than the time I had to get to class. I was using a camp stove to heat this reaction because we didn't have hot plates that went high enough yet, so I literally had to be there with it at all times. This is the email I sent to my prof: 'Hi Fr. Brian, is it okay if I zoom the class today? I encountered some poor planning on my part and began a reaction for my senior research that has to heat for 2 hours and I just can't leave it unattended. I was hoping I could just join the class remotely, so I can also avoid burning down Dupre. Thank you!' Dupre is our science building. He sent me the zoom link. We don't need any more fires at this school."*

- *"Yesterday while we were in a Zoom class, one of my students got a bat in her room and we all watched (transfixed and yelling encouragement) while her apartment maintenance dude ran around with a bag and a ladder trying to catch it."*

Now, students have had issues with online classes predating the pandemic, of course. However, as virtual classes have proliferated and become much more the norm over the past year or so, well so too have student "issues" with online classes:

- *"I will be unable to hear, and therefore participate in class for the first 8 weeks due to extensive ear piercing that prevents me wearing headphones. Also, I have no webcam or mic...I introduced this student to the office of disability services to see what tools they could provide to help her thrive. Suddenly, they found a speaker at home to at least be able to listen to class."* To which a heavily-pierced colleague replied: *"As someone with no less than 5 piercing in each ear, this person was truly full of it."*

- *"A student just told me he couldn't Zoom class because his car was stuck in the driveway due to snow. He has the internet at home and a laptop."*

- *"One of my final one-on-one Zoom critiques was interrupted by the student's maid wanting to clean their room."*

- *"I had a student say she couldn't complete her online work because she poked herself in the eye with a broom handle and couldn't see."*

- *"In the middle of a class one of my students' toddlers ran into the room naked and my student just slammed the computer shut and didn't come back. Later they emailed me and said 'I'm sorry for missing the remainder of class, I was too embarrassed to log back in after everyone saw my son's private parts.' I cackled and assured them it was okay."*

Finally, the online world has always been a place where students can do "interesting" things to cheat. This leads to the "cat and mouse" game of catching students cheating, but sometimes, students *can* make it easy, as the story from this anonymous colleague revealed with one of his student's online assignment submissions:

- *"In my former life, I got an email from the LMS tech support with an attached message from a student who had been buying alllll of his work from a pay site thinking the LMS tech email was the pay site email. He was basically chewing them out because 'his' work was late and it was going to affect 'his' grade.... He'd given them his login info and everything. They were posting discussions and papers, etc. Needless to say, he didn't graduate."*

Conclusion

Now while we may laugh at some of these online class-related excuses for their statistical unlikelihood and their absurdity, we all know that there are also excuses in this realm that are *both* absolutely true and in many cases, positively inspiring.

While we know that students have had a lot to deal with in the almost year that we have been living and learning with the COVID-19 pandemic, there are some REALLY inspiring stories to come out of all of this:

- *"I had a student who had a deportation scare and a mental health flare-up in the latter part of the semester at the beginning of the pandemic. She went from failing to passing, thanks to getting me all the missed work a few days after grade submission. Pretty impressive!"*

- *"I had a student cry today in a one-on-one Zoom call with me. I asked him why he didn't turn in his summary and he said when he reads his own words they look stupid. He is a refugee from Burma. I said I don't think he's stupid, I think he's doing something hard and brave and I'm proud of him, and I would love for him to think of himself that way. That's when he teared up."*

And yes, for all the complaining about Zoom courses - from both students and instructors - it is a platform that allows us to connect with each other wherever we are. Sometimes, this can lead to some unusual - and yes, inspirational - student stories, like this one:

- *"I had a student get on Zoom last spring while he was getting his hand stitched up (from nearly severing a finger) in the doctor's office."*

Chapter 14: The Travel File

In this chapter, we look at how travel issues - both real *and* imagined - have been used by students as an excuse for missing a class, a test, or a paper/project submission deadline, making for some very interesting excuses.

Travel Excuses

It may amaze folks outside of the academy that student travel plans - not for emergency travel for loved ones or close friends who were seriously ill or passed away - often serve as an "excuse," or are at least attempted to be used as such, by students today. Here is a sampling of travel-related excuses submitted by my contemporaries around the country:

- *"Would it be okay if I took the exam on another day because I went on vacation over the weekend and didn't have time to study."*

- *"Hi, I'm skiing in Vail for my mom's birthday, how can I make up today's class?"*

- *"'I couldn't handle it, it's just too much! I went to Mexico for some beach time.' Dude!"*

And maybe it's because I'm located just outside of New Orleans, meaning Orlando is within a day's drive or a one hour plane flight, but Disney trips seem to come-up quite often with students at my university. Yes, I have seen more than a few instances like this one reported by an anonymous colleague - *not* at my school!:

- *"I'm sorry I missed the due date. I went to Disney World."*

Here's a professor though who *definitely* wasn't a fan of Mickey Mouse:

- *"A student who 'informed' me they would be missing the final exam on the first day of class because of a family vacation to Disney. When I said that the final schedule is posted three years out and that that wasn't really an acceptable excuse in college their mom emailed me thinking I didn't believe the student or something. I had to reply that I couldn't even legally verify their child was in my course, but that if they were Disney wasn't an acceptable excuse..."*

Travel can lead to all sorts of interesting circumstances, although none may be more unlikely - but true - than this true story submitted for this project by one of my contemporaries:

- *"I had a student who sent me an email for a rest stop bathroom letting me know they would miss the exam. Somehow, the door lock broke and they were trapped. They sent me pics throughout the ordeal, including with the state trooper who kept them company while the county maintenance people were working."*

Now, a subset of travel-related issues is when students *actually* happen to get caught - either by happenstance *or* by a intrepid professor on the lookout for them - not really being away when they said they were traveling:

- *"My most favorite! Student emailed: 'I am sorry I couldn't make it to class, I missed my flight, I am at the airport....' I read this email as I saw him walking across campus. At the very least, hideout til class is over...."*

- *"I had a student once call to tell me he missed class because he was snowed in an hour away. This was in the days before everyone had cell phones. Caller ID told me he was calling from his dorm room!"*

And yes, travel can intersect with the current pandemic and virtual learning in weird and interesting ways indeed!:

- *"I had a student last semester in a remote class ask to take the final exam really early in the morning because he was at a ski resort and didn't want to have to come off the slopes in the middle of the day to take the exam. The entitlement if some of these students is insane - and don't go on a ski trip in the middle of a pandemic! (I teach at a university in Florida and he was an on-campus student, so no way it was a day trip and our county had very high levels of covid and I had multiple students test positive that semester). Ugh! I told him it was inappropriate to even ask me to get up super early and do a whole separate test just for him so he could ski an uninterrupted day."*

Conclusion

Now while we may laugh at some of these travel-related excuses for their statistical unlikelihood and their absurdity, we all know that there are also excuses in this realm that are *both* absolutely true and in many cases, positively inspiring.

Concerning travel issues, we know that there are indeed travel concerns that are *very real* for students. Here is an example of how students real life logistical issues made an impact on one professor:

- *"This is not a funny story, but was a wake up call for me. It was my first day teaching writing courses at a technical school near DC. 15 minutes before the class was scheduled to end, about half of the class suddenly packed up, stood up, and quietly left the room as I continued teaching. I stopped teaching and asked the remaining students what just happened. They told me that the students had to leave to catch the next bus, and if they didn't get that bus, they would have to wait another hour and would be late to work or other responsibilities. From then on, I ended the lecture portion of class early in anticipation of the early departures. I later learned that some students took three buses every day just to make it to class."*

Chapter 15: The "Better Options" File

In this chapter, we look at a unique area of excuses that have caused students to miss a class, a test, or a paper/project submission deadline. This area involves where students believed that they simply had a "better" option (meaning generally a more fun one) than being in class. In many cases as you will see, students may well be living better lives than their professors, but hey, we were young once too!

Better (More Fun) Options Than Being in Class

First off, let's be clear: *Your professors had fun in college, too!* And yes, our own fun experiences as students - some of which involved making the choice to pursue a "better option" than sitting in class on a specific day - can help shape how we look at the whole issue of what should be an excused or unexcused absence. Consider these reminiscences shared by two of my colleagues about their own experiences along these lines:

- *"When I did my Master's I missed a class because A-Ha was having a reunion concert that I would not miss! My instructor understood so now I try to be gracious and understanding with my students when there's something special going on in their lives—-excused absences shouldn't always be tragedies!"*

- *"Oh god, this reminded me of my own ridiculously lame excuse, that my teacher kindly accepted. I was about 21 (therefore technically a 'mature' first year student) at McGill. I ran into the Canadian folk superstars Spirit of the West and ended up spending the whole night hanging out with them across Montreal, taking in the sights and ending it with 5am poutine. I had a discussion paper due the next am in my cultural studies Film class. I told him the truth: 'I spent the night hanging out with SOTW and don't have my paper. Can I bring it tomorrow?' He said yes!"*

Sometimes, both professors *and* their students can look at the same event or activity and agree that yes, it is a "better option" than being in class (*well, part of a class maybe?*). But yes, sometimes faculty can move faster than their students in getting back from that fun "thing" happening, as this story submitted by one of my Boston contemporaries proves:

- *"I had students say they needed to miss class to go to the Red Sox victory parade and I said 'I'll prove that you can go to the parade and still get to class on time.' I went to the parade, posted pictures from the parade, headed to campus as soon as the team passed me, and got to class with 5 minutes to spare. They walked in 15 minutes later."*

And yes, a number of professors report students being very honest in that they simply had better - *read as more fun* - things to do than go to class! In fact, this area had a surprising number of *very* candid excuses shared by my colleagues from around America, centering on music, "work" events, and yes, sports!

Music

Now, being young once ourselves, we can relate to the importance of music and concerts (*remember those prior to the pandemic?*) in our lives. And so it is with today's students:

- *"My own recent annoyance was that a student felt she should get credit for a presentation she missed (her group presented without her) because she had tickets to a music festival. (class was on a weekday, but fest was on weekend). The joys of summer teaching."*

- *"Spice Girls concert! I excused the absence when she and several classmates she recruited sang and danced to a Spice Girls song."*

- *"I had a student tell me she wouldn't be able to attend the next day's class because Post Malone's new album was about to drop and 'that man just does something to me, so imma need some alone time.' My response was this: 'While I don't share your affinity for men with face tats, you haven't used any of your "freebie" absences ... so, enjoy!'"*

"Work" Events

More and more, students are simply not full-time, traditional students. And yes, that can lead to some "interesting" conflicts between their work and their class obligations today. Take for instance this one student, who obviously had a real conflict between not just her schooling, but between her main job as a teacher *and* her "side hustle":

- *"I had a student ask if she could miss a week of an accelerated (4 week) summer course because she 'had to' go to a Mary Kay Convention. LOL! P.S. It was a graduate-level course for middle school teachers!!!"*

Now whatever your political views may be, you have to admire students who want to be politically active, but... as an excuse for missing *half* the semester?:

- *"I had a student miss the first 7 weeks of the semester...his excuse was that he was campaigning for Obama."*

And yes today, wherever we teach, while we see students struggle financially, we always are likely to also have students in our classes who are probably far richer than we could ever dream to be:

- *"Student told me 'He had to open his restaurant in Las Vegas!'"*

Sports

As with the Boston Red Sox example discussed earlier, sports *does* create those "once in a lifetime" - or seemingly so - opportunities:

- *"The KC Royals won the World Series. I was teaching a graduate night class then and we are located close to St. Louis so there are a lot of baseball fans for the Cardinals and the Royals. A student emailed saying he had to go to KC and would have to miss class. Could he make up the quiz? Well I knew the parade was the day after my class so I was pretty sure it all had to do with baseball. So, I played a little, 'you can make up the quiz if you have a university approved absence or a funeral.' His answer, 'well technically I am going to the funeral of 30 years of bad baseball.'*

Bahahaha. I told him to go have fun and he can make up the quiz when he gets back."

- "I had a student call and ask if they could miss class for the class for the final four championship game - his Dad surprised him with tickets, I said 'of course.' I ended up with some neat championship apparel from the game. - and yes I absolutely accepted it!"

And then you could be this colleague of mine, who apparently is *the reason* for her school not having a lacrosse program that season, all because students took a Spring Break trip together to build that all important "team camaraderie" - and didn't bother to study for the test while in Cancun:

- "One semester about half of the lacrosse team was enrolled in my class. The class was part of the core curriculum so everyone at the university had to take it at some point. I had planned an exam for the Monday after Spring Break. I get to my office early on Monday morning and my inbox is stuffed full of late Sunday evening (and increasingly frantic) emails from students. A number of members of the lacrosse team had emailed me to inform me that they had just gotten back from Cancun and did not have enough time to 'cram' (they literally wrote that) for the exam. None of them showed up for the exam that morning. I have a very strict no make up exams without emergency documentation policy... unfortunately none of the team members had been doing fantastically well before they missed the exam. Every one of them ended up failing the class, and the following semester the university didn't have enough players not on academic suspension to have a lacrosse team that semester..."

Conclusion

Now while we may laugh at some of these "fun-related" excuses for their statistical unlikelihood and their absurdity, we all know that there are also excuses in this realm that are *both* absolutely true and in many cases, positively inspiring.

And when we look at the issue of students having "better options," sometimes better *does* mean more important things...like life experiences...

- *"Had a student miss an exam because he had to go to breakfast with Colin Powell. Sure, it dropped my jaw at the time. But teaching at George Washington U, I got used to it after a bit."*

... or small things that are indeed *far more* important family matters:

- *"Reminds me of when I was a PhD student and my husband was deployed. I asked to be excused from class so I could take my son trick-or-treating. Life happens. I'm glad I went out with my son."*

Chapter 16: The "Potpourri" File

In this chapter, we look at our final general area of excuses that have caused students to miss a class, a test, or a paper/project submission deadline. This general area is made up of anything *and* everything else, excuses submitted by my contemporaries across the country that didn't fit into one of the other more defined areas, like medical, tech, family, social, and of course, pet issues!

The Potpourri File

One thing is for certain: *There are simply great excuses among the many that my colleagues have submitted!* Take this one recounted by a professor from her father's college experience:

- *"My dad has a story that he once was late to class because he was listening to the song 'American Pie' for the first time on the radio. Once the prof heard the song, he excused the lateness!"*

And there are excuses that *no one* outside of academia would believe, but many of us on the inside can readily relate to, as yes, we've *all* encountered something along these lines before if we have taught for any length of time at all:

- *"I had a student who missed two weeks of class because he said he did not realize the semester had started."*

- *"One that comes to mind is that the student was not aware homework or assignments were required. Ever. Any. At any point."*

- *"I had a graduate student, who after week 3 and a no show, but still registered, say to me when I reached out to check: 'You mean I have to ATTEND classes?' This was a NYC teaching fellow."*

- *"A local student submitted an assignment an hour late and said she didn't know what time zone we lived in...all semester."*

- *"It's not fair to give me a low participation grade. I can't participate because I don't come to class."*

- *"I got lost between the parking lot and the classroom, so it was not worth coming."*

- *"I had a student write me 5 minutes before class began to say that he was really sorry for missing class but that he had forgotten to set his alarm."*

- *"On the first day of class, there was a sign on my classroom door indicating that a different class with a different instructor had moved to a new room. Apparently four students hung around the new room waiting for me. One of them emailed me and accused me of 'not showing up.'"*

Then, there is what I, myself, have found to be an extremely common one over the years, one that tells you, *"Hey, your stuff isn't as important to me as that other guy's!"*:

- *"I can't come to class next time - I have to study for a test in another class."*

Most of us can relate to having money problems at one point or another in our lives, and yes, college can be tough financially today! But, as the saying goes, money can't buy everything - and in this case, an excuse!:

- *"I had a student miss a major exam because he had to cash a check."*

Now elevators are a reality in any academic building today of two stories or more. And yes, they generate more than their share of student excuses:

- *"I got stuck in the elevator in our library once about fifteen minutes before my biology class started. I get an email on my phone from two students saying 'we're going to be late, we're stuck in an elevator.' I'm not sure what to say other than 'yeah I know, I'm literally in the same elevator.'"*

- *"Years ago, a student handed me a signed, sealed letter on letterhead in an official campus envelope. It was from the residence hall director, explaining that she had been trapped in an elevator during class."*

Yes, the arts are different. And there are different excuses for these kind of unique courses and their demands:

- *"Final painting critique; maid threw my paintings out."*

- *"Final scene in an acting one course: Student said: 'Someone drove their vehicle through the mall and I was traumatized by it. Can't do my scene!'"*

Then there's this one story about a student who *definitely* didn't get the memo that "the show must go on!":

- *"My hands-down favorite excuse comes from when I was teaching an acting class. The scene was from <u>Hamlet</u>. The actors are in place, the fencing moving forward, Gertrude collapsing with the cup when suddenly an agonized look of horror crosses the face of the student playing Claudius. 'Good, good!' I think. Claudius hasn't committed that much to this scene yet—this is a breakthrough moment...Instead, 'I can't die today' Claudius gasps, looking in horror around the dusty studio, 'I'm wearing Armani!'"*

And on a related note, clothing - or rather, the lack of availability of certain items - tended to be a common issue for students today...

- *"Student couldn't come to class because their dresser drawer broke and they had no pants. And had to wait for maintenance. I excused his absence."*

- *"'I don't have rain clothes' — this one made me wonder if what I was wearing was proper rain attire."*

- *"I had a student miss class because she 'could find tons of socks but no matches.'"*

Then there are excuses that spring from, well, *unusual* personal circumstances:

- *"I was once asked to remove certain assignments from a class because a student was in a beauty contest and had to spend extra time in a tanning salon."*

- *"'I couldn't do the assignment because I had to shave my body for the swim meet.' For me it was TMI."*

- *"I'm too pretty to attend clinical at that facility..."*

- *"The maid quit."*

Conclusion

Unlike most of the other chapters, this one doesn't conclude with a story of students persevering or overcoming adversity with such issues. Hopefully though, all of these students - and students in the future - will have learned from these experiences (and maybe even have a great story to tell about them someday!). I will conclude though with the excuse that was perhaps *the best* - or at least the most unusual - of the entire lot of submissions from the over 500 professors who contributed to this project:

- *"A student was 5 minutes late for the beginning of an exam. When they walked in, they immediately apologized: 'I am so sorry I am late, I was being chased by a zombie.' I handed them the exam, no questions asked. I figured it was creative enough to warrant a pass. After class the student confirmed that it was real - some people were dressed up as zombies to promote something (blood drive I think?), and they were friends of his who temporarily delayed his trip to class."*

And yes, then there's the *perfect* retort we wish we could all say to a student who mysteriously shows up at the end of the semester after being mysteriously absent for some time:

- *"Student strolls in after 3 weeks absent....says: 'Oh, my bad...I just needed some time off. Can I get the final?' I simply responded: 'No, dude!'"*

Chapter 17: Conclusion

Wow! I hope you enjoyed this unique book! If so, please share it with/ recommend it to your friends, colleagues, and yes, maybe even your students!

In concluding this entire project, I must again express my gratitude to the over 500 of my fellow professors who took the time to share their thoughts on their students' excuses with me for this project. *Literally*, what you have read in this book would not have been possible without each of them taking the time to provide the input that became, what I think, is a very interesting compendium of the many, *many* types of excuses that college faculty hear - routinely or not-so-routinely - from students today. Many of you reading this book may not be surprised at all at what you have read, while some of you may be aghast at just how far today's college students will go - *and* how creative they can be - in concocting excuses to get out of being in class, missing a test, or being late for an assignment/project deadline.

Some of you may also have been very surprised at the candor displayed by students in relating - sometimes with way, *way* too much information - as to why they could not be in class, miss a test, be late on a project/paper, etc. for *whatever* the reason. But this is the wider world in which we live today, and by default, this *is* the world in which higher education exists today. So while some may pine for the "good old days" when simply saying you had a "stomach bug" was the catch-all excuse for *whatever* might have kept you from going to class, yes, today we can have hard-to-believe stories backed-up by pictures - and even video - from the latest iPhone in the student's pocket! Of course, those same "impossible, but true" tales from students might be contradicted by simply scrolling Instagram or other social media and seeing where the student who claimed to be sick, out-of-town, or even grieving was out having fun! The technology *does* indeed work both ways today!

Speaking directly to the students who have read this book, as I've stated repeatedly throughout the chapters in this book, college faculty are, by and large, a very empathetic *and* understanding group of individuals. After all, to a person, they have made a career choice to work with students just like yourself. So, while no profession has people who are 100% alike, college professors and instructors are generally people who will be willing to work with you *whatever* your concerns might be. However, as a student, you should approach them with a degree of respect and professionalism befitting their attainment, and that begins with being honest in the information you are trying to convey to them.

So, after spending over thirty years in the college classroom myself and having spent a good amount of time learning how my colleagues have approached the whole issue of student excuses - from health matters to simply having better options than being in class - *even before* this project came about, I have to end this book with my best bit of advice for students, and it is simple. When it comes to excuses, honesty is always - *always* - the best approach! This one excuse story that was shared by a colleague earlier in the chapter on excuses caused by "friends" is certainly, in the end, a positive one, as while it deals with alcohol use (or misuse), the honesty shown by this student is indeed commendable:

- "I had a student come apologize for missing the previous class. They looked me right in the eye and said, 'I turned 21 the night before and I was so hungover. The shape I was in, my presence would have been a disrespect to you and your class.' They were clear they weren't trying to get the absence excused. They believed in always telling the truth, but wanted to be clear they took the class seriously. I will never forget that unabashed, yet entirely respectful honesty."

I can safely say both from my own experience and the experiences of the hundreds of fellow faculty members who contributed their thoughts and insights to this project, your desire as a student for a "helping hand" is enhanced by doing so *genuinely*. On the other hand, once you begin to come across as being disingenuous and perhaps even dishonest with your excuse, you *dramatically* lower the odds of getting whatever it is you might want from sharing the reason for your missed class, test, or deadline. It may be a cliche, but at the end of the day, honesty *is* the best policy! As in any relationship, once you lose trust, the relationship is hard to recover. So, I would urge students to think about this when confronting that "moment of truth" about whether to concoct a "great" excuse or to simply tell the truth to their professor or instructor. I can say confidently that the latter approach is the best one for you to take! And yes as student, you might be surprised that an honest, "non-excuse excuse" might work better than even the most creative one you could come up with, as this final story shared by a colleague proves:

- *"I had a student email me: 'I have no good excuse and I'd rather not have to explain my bad reasons. I will turn in all of my late assignments by the end of the week. If you have time to evaluate them I'd appreciate feedback, even though I don't expect to receive credit.' I appreciated their honesty and humility!"*

However, I do not doubt that right now, there are students who are staying up late to think about the next great excuse they can use or just scrambling five minutes before class with what they should email or tell their professor about being absent or missing a test that day! So yes, *there could be a sequel to this project to come!* And so if you are a faculty member, please send your latest, greatest student excuses to my email at dwyld@selu.edu - and yes, I will use everyone's excuses *anonymously* in any future projects.

About the Author

David Wyld (dwyld@selu.edu) serves as the Merritt Professor of Strategic Management at Southeastern Louisiana University in Hammond, Louisiana. Dr. Wyld is the founder and publisher of both <u>Modern Business Press</u> (*publishing leading-edge academic journals*) and <u>The IDEA Publishing</u> (*publishing articles of interest across a wide variety of topics, giving both newbie authors and content marketers a platform for their ideas*). As a prolific writer himself, he is a frequent contributor to both respected academic journals and widely read trade and general interest publications. He has established himself as one of the leading academic experts on emerging applications of technology in both the private and public sectors. Dr. Wyld continues to be an active strategic management consultant, a qualified expert witness, and invited speaker on a wide variety of topics to trade, corporate, governmental, and academic audiences. He has made appearances on management and technology issues on The Discovery Channel, ESPN Radio, Federal News Radio, and other media outlets.

Dr. Wyld has earned Southeastern's President's Award for both Excellence in Teaching and Research, making him one of a select group of faculty who have been awarded campus-wide recognition for more than one aspect of the professorial role. He earned his doctorate from the University of Memphis in 1993.

You can view his complete academic vita at https://davidcwyld.blogspot.com.

Social Media Links to David Wyld:

- on Facebook[1]
- on LinkedIn[2]
- on Medium[3]

---

1.   https://www.facebook.com/david.wyld

2.   https://www.linkedin.com/in/david-wyld-4923707/

3.   https://davidwyld.medium.com/

About the Author

David C. Wyld currently serves as the Merritt Professor of Management at Southeastern Louisiana University in Hammond, Louisiana.

Read more at https://www.linkedin.com/in/david-wyld-4923707/.

www.ingramcontent.com/pod-product-compliance
Lightning Source LLC
Chambersburg PA
CBHW051245160726
47994CB00003B/1030